Samuel Barber Remembered

Eastman Studies in Music

Ralph P. Locke, Senior Editor
Eastman School of Music

Additional Titles on Music of the Twentieth Century

A complete list of titles in the Eastman Studies in Music Series,
in order of publication, may be found on our website, www.urpress.com.

Samuel Barber
Remembered

A Centenary Tribute

EDITED BY PETER DICKINSON

R UNIVERSITY OF ROCHESTER PRESS

First published 2010

University of Rochester Press
668 Mt. Hope Avenue, Rochester, NY 14620, USA
www.urpress.com
and Boydell & Brewer Limited
PO Box 9, Woodbridge, Suffolk IP12 3DF, UK
www.boydellandbrewer.com

ISBN-13: 978-1-58046-350-8
ISSN: 1071-9989

Library of Congress Cataloging-in-Publication Data

Samuel Barber remembered : a centenary tribute / edited by Peter Dickinson.
    p. cm. — (Eastman studies in music, ISSN 1071-9989 ; v. 74)
  Includes bibliographical references and index.
  ISBN 978-1-58046-350-8 (hardcover : alk. paper)
1. Barber, Samuel, 1910–1981. 2. Barber, Samuel, 1910–1981—Interviews.
3. Musicians—Interviews. I. Dickinson, Peter.
  ML410.B23S35   2010
  780.92—dc22
  [B]

                                          2009047684

A catalogue record for this title is available from the British Library.

This publication is printed on acid-free paper.
Printed in Great Britain by CPI Antony Rowe Ltd, Chippenham and Eastbourne

Contents

Illustrations

Foreword

John Corigliano

It is impossible to evaluate the true worth of composers when they are alive because their works are not heard as pure music but rather as political statements by their creators. Today, when they are still alive, self-consciously modern and would-be progressive composers are often elevated to great heights in our cultural conversation regardless of the actual quality of their musical imaginations. In the past, this was not the case. As a result, composers more talented than radical, who are interested in the new only insofar as it relates to the good, are pigeonholed into the "traditional" or "conservative" categories. The quality of the work matters less than what it represents in the current discourse. Barber was of the latter kind and was stereotyped accordingly.

During his lifetime, people who liked "old-fashioned music" liked him; people who liked "modernist and experimental" music did not. Ironically, even Barber himself succumbed to this if-new-then-good dogma. He once told me that during his student days at the Curtis Institute, he and his composing friends used to sit in the balcony listening to premieres of Rachmaninoff with disdain. "How foolish I was then," he sighed.

I sent Sam a copy of my chorus and orchestra setting of Dylan Thomas's "Fern Hill," at that time for chorus and piano, and he liked it and gave it to Schirmer. He made one or two suggestions—mainly cutting a measure or two to dovetail a transition or changing one note he thought clumsy—but said he was sincerely impressed. For many years afterward I showed him my works before sending them on to Hans Heinsheimer, Schirmer's legendary publisher.

Fortunately, the minute a composer passes away, his place on the artistic/political chessboard vanishes with him. Shostakovich, for example, when alive, was considered too cheap, too vulgar to be respected. But his music has survived, while the disdain for it has not. Shostakovich is now considered a great composer by the very people who dismissed him when he was writing. Barber, now gone, is appreciated as a master and grouped with the great composers of the past. Nobody cares whether his music was groundbreaking, like Berlioz's, or not, like Mozart's. And so we are free to listen to a true musician writing eternal music. Barber would have loved that!

About the 1981 BBC Interviews

ARTHUR JOHNSON

The advent of this book brings to a conclusion a series of events that began shortly before Samuel Barber's death in 1981. The previous year the record company Hyperion invited my wife—the pianist Angela Brownridge—to record his complete published piano music, an LP that was released the week Barber died.[1]

As a music producer with BBC Radio 3, I had already proposed a documentary program on Barber's life and work, but the idea was slow to get off the ground because his reputation with the British musical establishment at that time was not particularly strong. In addition, Barber had little personal contact with the British Isles. At first there was some reluctance by the BBC to make the program, but when the news arrived of Barber's death, any uncertainty gracefully waned.

In the 1970s and 1980s, BBC Radio 3 was a stimulating cultural environment—a period now sometimes referred to nostalgically as the "Golden Years." Demands placed on producers were often great, but in the case of such programs as documentaries, although pre-commission scrutiny was severe, once all that was over the producer was simply left to get on with it.

Arthur Johnson began his career in the record industry before joining the BBC where he was a music program producer for twenty-three years, finally occupying the post of program editor. He managed to expand greatly the output of music documentaries from the music department, including two others with Peter Dickinson that dealt with the British composers Sir Lennox Berkeley and Lord Berners. *Lennox Berkeley*, broadcast on BBC Radio 3, August 31, 1992, repeated on September 13, 1994; *Lord Berners*, BBC Radio 3, September 18, 1983, Sony Radio Awards 1984 Certificate of Commendation in the category of Best Radio Features Programme, repeated January 3, 1985.

1. *The Piano Music of Samuel Barber*, Angela Brownridge, Hyperion A66016 (1980), CDH 88016. Angela Brownridge was a soloist in concertos throughout the UK and Europe in her early teens. She won a piano scholarship to the University of Edinburgh and studied privately with Guido Agosti in Rome and Maria Curcio in London. In addition to her reputation as a soloist, she has also lectured in the United States on the music of Samuel Barber.

The most important task was to find a presenter, not always easy in the musical climate described. Fortunately, I had come across someone with attractive qualifications: a composer-musician with a background of study in the United States, a fluent writer, and a proven communicator. But there was one problem: Peter Dickinson, founder and head of the Music Department and its Centre for American Music at the University of Keele (1974–84), was a busy professor of music at one of the country's well-established universities and might not be sympathetic to the idea of undertaking a thorough study of the life and work of Samuel Barber. I seem to remember that it took three phone calls before I finally persuaded him to take on the job. Strangely enough, I now believe it was that initial quality of the Doubting Thomas that provided the signature to the conversations that form this book. Throughout the extensive course of interviews, Dickinson continually impressed me with the depth of his background knowledge and his ability to pose contrasting points of view—techniques of interviewing that could have been less forthcoming from one more comfortable with the subject but conducted here with considerable aplomb. That, of course, is to oversimplify the matter. Suffice it to say that in these pages we have preserved the views and recollections of several of the twentieth century's great musical figures, views and recollections that should contribute moreover to an appreciation of the life of Samuel Barber and the lasting value of his music.

Acknowledgments

This book started with the initiative of the British Broadcasting Corporation, represented by Arthur Johnson, producer of our one-hour Radio 3 documentary *Samuel Barber (died 23 January 1981),* broadcast on January 23, 1982 and repeated on May 1, 1982. The first broadcast was followed by the British premiere of Barber's Canzonetta for Oboe and Piano played by Sarah Francis and me.[1] I owe an enormous amount to Johnson's enthusiasm for Barber and am also grateful to Jacqueline Kavanagh, written archivist of the BBC, for permission to use the interviews; I hereby make full acknowledgment. This is the third monograph I have based on BBC interviews, fully annotated with additional discussion. The others are *CageTalk: Dialogues with and about John Cage* (Rochester, NY: University of Rochester Press, 2006) and *Lord Berners: Composer, Writer and Painter* (Woodbridge, Suffolk: Boydell, 2008). As in these books, my editorial method involved transcribing all the interviews, then cutting repetitions in the answers, removing or correcting occasional factual errors, and condensing the questions asked to make a readable narrative.

The main purpose of this book, which is timed as a centenary tribute, is to make these historic interviews available in their complete form for the first time. Scholars will need the information contained here, and the general reader who enjoys Barber's music should find new insights. The circumstances of Barber's life have been outlined by both Nathan Broder[2] and Barbara Heyman.[3] Heyman's *Comprehensive Catalog of the Complete Works of Samuel Barber* will be an essential resource when it appears, as will the new edition of her authoritative biography. Monographs about Menotti have provided further insight into the lives of the two composers, so closely linked for most of their personal and professional lives. The new interviews with friends, composers, performers, publishers, and critics in this collection—recorded mostly in 1981—provide further detail from some who knew Barber in various capacities. Then, when I was honored to be invited by the Samuel Barber Foundation to give a lecture on Barber at the First

1. The British premiere of the orchestral version was given by Sarah Francis with the Academy of London under Richard Stamp at the Queen Elizabeth Hall on November 29, 1982.

2. Nathan Broder, *Samuel Barber* (New York: G. Schirmer, 1954).

3. Barbara B. Heyman, *Samuel Barber: The Composer and His Music* (New York: Oxford University Press, 1992).

Presbyterian Church in West Chester, Pennsylvania, on October 12, 2005, I also had the chance to meet and interview Orlando Cole in Philadelphia. He was an exact contemporary of Barber's at the Curtis Institute and proved remarkably lively in his mid-nineties. After my lecture I gave what must have been the first performance of Barber's last work, the Canzonetta for Oboe and Piano, in my version for piano solo.

In 1981 and early 1982, a few months after I conducted my own interviews for the BBC Radio 3 documentary, Brent D. Fegley, then a student at West Chester State College and now at the University of Illinois, interviewed thirteen people in West Chester who had known Barber and his family. Some of these people were of advanced age, struggling to recall distant events. Fegley also met Menotti, and details from that interview are noted within my interview with him that follows. Some of Fegley's discussions were more concerned with local history in West Chester than with music, but they all throw varied light on Barber's background and provide reminiscences not otherwise available. I am grateful to Fegley for transcribing his interviews, which made it possible for me to rescue extracts included in chapter 1. Fortunately, Professor Sterling Murray retained Fegley's work and Major Frank Hudson also helped with transcriptions. I am particularly grateful to Ulrich Klabunde, most recently of the Samuel Barber Foundation, for his constant support over several years in giving me access to these interviews and arranging a grant toward publication now generously provided by the Samuel Barber Fund at the West Chester University Foundation.

My discussion of Barber's reception in England covers the British response in the years before, during, and after World War II. It reveals the climate in which Barber's reputation gradually soared, apart from a period during the 1960s when any composer adhering too closely to traditional techniques was regarded as suspect by the professional musical establishment. In his foreword, John Corigliano notes the way such discrimination has operated. I enjoyed a telephone conversation with Natasha Litvin, Sir Stephen Spender's widow, who played the Barber Piano Sonata in London in 1951 and remembered visiting Barber and Menotti at Mt. Kisco in the late 1940s.

I record my grateful thanks to Tom Bartunek, general manager of WQXR, for permission to print the two radio interviews with Barber; Francis Menotti for his father's interview; Jessica Rauch for dealing with permissions from the Aaron Copland Fund and the Virgil Thomson Foundation; Anthony Schuman for his father's interview; Leontyne Price, who saw a copy of her interview and confirmed her approval through her brother Gen. George Price; Elizabeth Witchey-Ryer for the interview with her late brother John Browning; Robert White, who saw his interview with Arthur Johnson and helped me with further contacts and a photograph; Janet Hitchcock for the interview with her late husband, H. Wiley Hitchcock, whose encouragement and friendship I was fortunate to enjoy for over thirty years; Frances Heinsheimer Wainwright for her father's interview; Edward Murphy who saw his interview; Orlando Cole for being prepared to be interviewed, and Jennifer Rycerz at the Curtis Institute, who arranged that interview through Ulrich Klabunde; and Thomas Winters, who recorded it.

All attempts to reach Charles Turner's executors have failed—even the Estates and Claims Department at ASCAP cannot trace them—but, in view of his approval of the BBC Radio 3 documentary quoted from his letters to me in the introduction to the interview, I am certain he would have wanted his contribution to appear with the others.

Peggy Monastra at Schirmer has given generously of her time in coping with my inquiries and has provided all the photographs, with the assistance of Michael McCurdy, apart from the picture of Barber's grave taken by Ulrich Klabunde. I have shared material with David Perkins and with Pierre Brévignon in Paris, where he has started a Samuel Barber Society. I made all these interviews available to Brévignon in advance, and his French biography will be of great interest. Assistance also came from Nicholas Clark at the Britten-Pears Library, Aldeburgh; James Wintle at the Library of Congress, Washington, DC; Jeni Dahmus, archivist at the Juilliard School of Music; and Betty Jacobs, who gave me access to the recordings owned by her late husband, the writer and critic Arthur Jacobs. Vivian Perlis helped me with contacts and support for my American music activities over many years. I owe much to the initiative of Keele University, Staffordshire, where I started the Music Department with its Centre for American Music program and ran it from 1974 to 1984. My colleagues were fully supportive, especially the late Norman Josephs, Stephen Banfield, and William Brooks as a Visiting Fulbright-Hays Professor. Looking even further back, I might never have become interested in American music if my father, contact-lens pioneer Frank Dickinson (1906–78), had not encouraged me to apply for a Rotary Foundation fellowship that enabled me to do postgraduate study in the United States, where I attended the Juilliard School of Music in New York City.

I have also valued my contact with Suzanne Guiod and Ralph Locke at the University of Rochester Press and the team there as well as the encouragement of Peter Clifford and Bruce Phillips at Boydell in England. Arthur Johnson not only started the whole project in 1980 but transcribed several of the interviews twenty-seven years later when he was struggling against very poor health. I shared the typescript first with my wife, Bridget, who read it and made valuable suggestions. Then it was seen in whole or in part by Barbara Heyman, Nancy and Ulrich Klabunde, and Arnold Whittall, who all made suggestions.

I am also grateful for the support of Rochester's anonymous readers who helped to focus the book and especially to Cheryl Carnahan, my fastidious copy-editor for both *CageTalk* and this book.

Peter Dickinson
Aldeburgh, Suffolk, 2009

Part One

Peter Dickinson on
Samuel Barber

Chapter One

The Formative Years

PETER DICKINSON

Samuel Osborne Barber II—the full name the composer later gave up—was born on March 9, 1910, at 35 South High Street, West Chester, near Philadelphia. His paternal grandfather, the first Samuel O. Barber, was a manufacturer of shipping tags who had moved to West Chester in 1888 with the Denny Tag Company. He set up his own highly successful firm, the Keystone Tag Company, in 1901, which the family ran until 1941. The composer's maternal grandfather was a Presbyterian minister, Dr. William Trimble Beatty, who founded Shady Side Presbyterian Church in Pittsburgh. He was also instrumental in founding the Pennsylvania College for Women. He died at only age forty-eight and left his widow with eight children; they moved to West Chester in 1885.

Helen John was in high school with Barber and recalled, "West Chester was plainer than most towns, quite strict with a strong Quaker influence."[1] One of the Beatty children became the famous opera singer Louise Homer.[2] Her husband, Sidney Homer, recalled that West Chester "was the most retired retiring town one could imagine. Even the houses seemed to retire behind the massive maple trees. So quiet were the streets that when you walked you walked softly, if you had to speak you spoke softly."[3] Louise Homer's younger sister was Barber's mother, Marguerite McLeod Beatty, known as Daisy. Ruth

---

1. Helen John, interview with Peter Dickinson, West Chester, PA, October 12, 2005. Further interviews with Barber's contemporaries found in *Samuel Barber: Portrait of a Musical Master,* by the Henderson High School American History Seminar, West Chester Area School District, 1982–83, confirm the impressions given here. See there Carolyn S. Neary, "Samuel Barber: An Oral Recollection," 23–30; available at www.samuelbarber.fr.

2. Louise Homer, née Louise Dilworth Beatty (1871–1947), studied in Philadelphia and Boston, where she met and married Sidney Homer (1864–1953). They moved to Paris so she could continue her studies and begin her career. Her U.S. debut was in 1900; she remained a leading operatic contralto with opera companies in New York, Chicago, San Francisco, and Los Angeles until her stage retirement in 1929. She was acclaimed as Dalilah to Caruso's Samson in Saint-Saëns's opera. See Sidney Homer, *My Wife and I* (New York: Macmillan, 1939).

3. Ibid., 127.

Dean, a neighbor, recalled that all the Beattys had fine singing voices.[4] They were descendants of the inventor Robert Fulton (1765–1815), who developed steamboats and an early submarine. There was less music on the Barber side of the family, although Ada Strode, Samuel's aunt, was a piano teacher.

Samuel Le Roy Barber, the composer's father, married Daisy on October 17, 1905, in the First Presbyterian Church, West Chester. The couple had two children. Samuel Barber grew up close to his sister, Sara Fulton Barber (1913–61). She sang beautifully, and it was a great loss when she died prematurely of asthma. Roy Barber was a doctor, widely respected in the small-town community where everybody knew each other's religion and politics. As Henry James explained: "This profession in America has constantly been held in honor, and more successfully than elsewhere has put forward a claim to the epithet of 'liberal.' In a country in which, to play your social part, you must either earn your income or make believe that you earn it, the healing art has appeared in a high degree to combine two recognized sources of credit. It belongs to the realm of the practical . . . and is touched by the light of science."[5]

In 1902, Roy Barber graduated from the Hahneman Medical School in Philadelphia as a homeopathic doctor, and he was in general practice as well as a surgeon. He was a member of the Rotary Club of West Chester and the West Chester Lodge and was president of the board of the First Presbyterian Church. He was known to be generous toward patients who couldn't afford to pay. Unlike his son, he was keen on sports; and he was not overly awed by the celebrities who later came to the house. A neighbor recalled: "Dr. Barber was a handsome man, not terribly tall, but a fine doctor who had lots of patients in West Chester. People liked him very much . . . he was very gracious to everybody. Mrs. Barber was delightful. She was in the women's organizations in the town—a very nice person."[6] But the daughter of the Barbers' housekeeper thought "Mrs. Barber was hard to get acquainted with. Lots of people in town will tell you that, but I never had trouble with her. She had very poor eyesight and she could pass you on the street. If you didn't say hello to her . . . she wouldn't see you."[7] Her most absorbing interest was her children and their activities, and the Barbers were part of a close-knit group of families. They supported the First Presbyterian Church, where Mrs. Barber was a Sunday School teacher. Dr. Barber was chair of the West Chester School Board for twenty-five years; it was in that capacity that he ruled that any student who was a composer could take Fridays off from school to go to Philadelphia Orchestra concerts, which Mrs. Barber attended regularly.[8]

---

4. Ruth Dean, interview with Brent D. Fegley, December 3, 1981.

5. Henry James, *Washington Square* (New York: Harper and Brothers, 1880), opening paragraph.

6. Mrs. Swope, interview with Brent D. Fegley, November 23, 1981.

7. Marie Brosius, interview with Brent D. Fegley, January 23, 1982.

8. Nathan Broder, *Samuel Barber* (New York: G. Schirmer, 1954), 12.

One of Barber's cousins described the economic position of such families:

> We were upper-middle class, as it were . . . in the lower echelons of wealth per se. . . . We were all sent to private schools and college and we lived nicely. We didn't have yachts and things like that . . . but we had help in our maids, cooks, cleaning women, laundresses . . . and our mothers played bridge in the afternoon and went to luncheons. . . . We belonged to the golf club, played golf and tennis and swam at Brinton's Quarry. They were lovely days. You didn't do your own carrying wood or splitting it! My grandchildren have no conception of how we lived on [just] a few thousand dollars a year![9]

Another cousin remembered that the children had a wonderful time at their grandfather's tag factory long before health and safety became concerns:

> We'd play hide-and-seek in the stockroom where all the rolls of tag paper were and the people that worked there were terribly nice to us. . . . There'd be lovely lacey bits of paper coming off the machine that punched out the tags and we'd gather those up off the floor . . . we thought they were beautiful. . . . We all put strings in the tags. Grandfather used to bring boxes home—they were all strung by hand in those days. We weren't good enough to do the wire ones but we all got boxes of tags and you got ten cents a box as I remember.[10]

Apparently Sam had a nursemaid and "was always singing."[11] His mother, who played the piano, had a horror of amateur male pianists, so Sam was started on the cello, although he soon moved to the piano.[12] Anna L. Baker, who knew Samuel as a child, remembered "a boy in third grade . . . at a Christmas performance for the parents," when he was "lifted up on a chair in order to play his little cello."[13]

From around age nine, the boy had a remarkable sense of his destiny. He left a note for his mother that read:

> Dear Mother: I have written this to tell you my worrying secret. Now don't cry when you read it because it is neither yours nor my fault. I suppose I shall have to tell it now without any nonsense. To begin with I was not meant to be an athlete. I was meant to be a composer, and will be I'm sure. I'll ask you one more thing—don't ask me to try and forget this unpleasant thing and go

---

9. Mrs. Swope, interview with Fegley.

10. Mrs. Strickland, interview with Brent D. Fegley, January 9, 1982.

11. Mrs. Swope, interview with Fegley.

12. Broder, *Samuel Barber*, 10.

13. Anna L. Baker, interview with Brent D. Fegley, November 24, 1981.

play football. *Please*—Sometimes I've been worrying about this so much that it makes me mad (not very).

Love, Sam Barber II[14]

It appears that the Barbers' Irish housekeeper, Annie Sullivan Brosius, was a significant influence on Sam as a child. Brosius sang Irish songs, played dances and jigs on the accordion, and told young Sam fairy tales in the kitchen.[15] In 1958 Barber recalled: "She had been sent over from Ireland by my grandmother. Whenever she and my mother had a misunderstanding and my mother threatened to dismiss her, she would simply inform my mother that she was older, had been in the family longer, and would not go. She had an unlimited collection of Irish songs in her repertoire."[16] She provided the libretto for the first act of an unfinished opera *The Rose Tree,* which Barber set at age ten—part of a large juvenilia. The heroine's part was written for his sister who told Nathan Broder in 1954 that she could still sing every note.[17]

There was family music making, especially when the Homers traveled up from Florida and stopped off at West Chester. Pierre DuPont, who ran the Longwood Conservatory at his country estate, supported Barber locally as a boy and introduced him to John Philip Sousa after a concert.[18] A cousin remembered one special occasion:

> Longwood Gardens was open to the public every other Sunday and then there were the private Sundays on alternate weeks. . . . When Louise Homer was here Mr. DuPont always loved seeing her, and my family was invited with the Barber family . . . and there was no one else there. . . . Sam played the organ and Louise Homer sang some of her favorite songs . . . and then some arias from her favorite operas. I was very impressed: she was so lovely. She wore a navy blue—I guess you would call it in those days—traveling dress and Mr. DuPont clipped off a beautiful long-stemmed, deep red rosebud and Aunt Louise held that in her hand and stood in the Conservatory, Sam playing the organ, and sang. . . . I remember how much I loved her singing that Sunday.[19]

---

14. Cited in Barbara B. Heyman, *Samuel Barber: The Composer and his Music* (New York: Oxford University Press, 1992), 7.

15. Brosius, interview with Fegley. In the interview Brosius mentions that Barber gave a magazine interview about her mother-in-law, Annie Brosius.

16. Emily Coleman, "The Composer Talks with Emily Coleman . . . Samuel Barber and *Vanessa,*" *Theatre Arts* (January 1958): 68–69, 86–88. Barber described her as the family's cook and called her Annie Brosius Sullivan Noble.

17. Broder, *Samuel Barber,* 11.

18. Pierre DuPont was head of the DuPont Company and president and chairman of General Motors. He grew flowers, fruit, and vegetables at the Longwood Conservatory, which housed the organ Barber played. The Conservatory, now part of the Longwood Foundation, is still the setting for musical and social events and world-famous horticultural displays.

19. Mrs. Strickland, interview with Fegley.

When Louise Homer sang with the Metropolitan Opera in Philadelphia, she sent tickets for a box to the families in West Chester.

The boy's contemporary, Robert S. Gawthrop, who practiced as a lawyer in West Chester, related that his family was friendly with the Barbers and that they went on holidays together, usually in the Pocono Mountains. Sam, he said, was "a little bit different . . . was not the boy who was round playing baseball or shooting marbles."[20]

But Barber did have high school friends who were not closely involved with music. Ruth Dean identified William Snyder, who may have gone into the navy; William Palmer Lear, who became head of the art department in the [local] public schools; and Edward Dicks, whom Barber also used to see in New York.[21] Gawthrop said: "He [Barber] was brilliant and his whole life was music. . . . He'd rather sit, maybe practice or listen to music than anything else. . . . He did play sports and things but was more interested in music than [in] going around like young fellows did. . . . You could tell he was an artist of some kind."[22] Others confirmed that Barber was not interested in games, not even card games.[23] According to Bill Brosius, "If Sam liked you he really liked you. If he didn't he didn't want to be bothered. . . . I noticed that in his life here, even when he was a little boy."[24]

At high school Barber was a year ahead of his class and "a nice young boy, always smiling, happy, well-liked . . . jolly and friendly. Everybody knew Sam: he knew almost everything about music as far as we were concerned."[25] Gawthrop said his classmates were surprised when Sam once played the saxophone in the high school orchestra. When the circus came to town in about 1926, he became a star:

> The circus coming to West Chester was quite different in those days from what it is today [1981]. It came by train and on the train were the big circus wagons with the caged animals and the calliope. They'd pull the carriages down the street in their rather gaudy parade—really quite a function in a quiet little town like this! We'd get up there early in the morning and watch them unload. . . . When Sam went down to the place where they were unloading he immediately went over to where the steam-driven calliope was. . . . Sam pretty soon demonstrated his ability to the man who rode the calliope and when it came down Market Street in West Chester . . . there wasn't any painted clown

20. Robert S. Gawthrop, interview with Brent D. Fegley, January 19, 1982.

21. Dean, interview with Fegley.

22. Gawthrop, interview with Fegley.

23. However, friends of Barber in his later years told his biographer, Barbara Heyman, that he was an avid bridge player. E-mail from Heyman to me, July 13, 2009.

24. Bill Brosius, interview with Brent D. Fegley, January 23, 1982.

25. John, interview with Dickinson.

or paid operator from the circus operating it but old Sam. So that's another instrument I heard him play![26]

Barber was also organist at Westminster Church in West Chester in his early teens, although he held the post for less than a year. However, "He always played the organ for Children's Day at the Presbyterian Church. . . . The rehearsals were such fun because we got there before the choir director and Sam would play all kinds of popular music on the organ. . . . When you heard the director approaching, Sam would go right into something that belonged in the church and we'd all giggle and laugh as we were smaller children. . . . He had a sense of humor and was very well liked. Nothing aloof or superior or high hat—that's a good old-fashioned expression—about him."[27]

The 1926 commencement issue of the high school yearbook reported on Barber: "Since his freshman year, whenever an interesting program was desired, Sam was called upon to preside at the piano. He was not content to play compositions of others, but entranced his audience by playing many of his own. He was not only accomplished in music, but [also] in Latin and French classes where, whenever a difficult passage is reached, we turn to Sam who translates this for us in a manner that shows us the beauty of the languages."[28]

Helen John and Barber were in a classical course in high school that consisted of Latin and French, preparatory to college. John remembered first being aware of Barber when they both had parts in a French play at school that had six characters. He was sixteen: she was seventeen. He acted and also played the piano—the music was the old folk tune "Sur le pont d'Avignon." Performed in French, the play was called *L'Abbé Constantin*.[29] John called it "a Catholic play" in which she played the mother; the priest was played by a girl who wore a black graduation outfit; and Barber played the son. As the mother, John was there to defend her son because she thought "the priest had something against him."[30]

---

26. Gawthrop, interview with Fegley. The calliope is an instrument operated by steam or compressed air and designed for use outdoors, associated with fairgrounds and riverboats. It was invented by John C. Stoddard of Worcester, Massachusetts, and launched in 1855. Barber would have played a portable type with a keyboard usually capable of simple textures in two parts.

27. Mrs. Strickland, interview with Fegley.

28. From a copy located by Charles Zook, who was in the same class as Barber; interview with Brent D. Fegley, November 5, 1981.

29. A comedy in three acts drawn from the novel of that name by Ludovic Halévy (1834–1908). The novel was extremely popular when it came out in 1882 and was regularly reprinted. As a result, Halévy was elected to the Académie francaise in 1884. The adaptation for the stage was made in 1891 by Hector Jonathan Crémieux and Pierre Recourcell. Halévy and H. Meilhac were responsible for the libretto based on Merimée for Bizet's *Carmen* (1875), as well as for libretti of operas by Offenbach.

30. John, interview with Dickinson.

Raymond Henry was a fellow student of Barber's piano teacher, William Hatton Green, and provided extraordinary detail about a remarkable musician who had the strongest influence on Barber until he went to the Curtis Institute:

> William Hatton Green was the son of a printer in Philadelphia, and when the printing business got bad his father told him he had to go out and make a living for himself—which he hadn't done at thirty-three years of age. He had a friend who was a pianist so he started on the keyboard, never having played previously. He went to Europe, came back with about 150 compositions at his fingertips, made tours, and made quite a large sum of money out of it. Then he settled down in West Chester and taught music for years both here and in Germantown.

Green was a pupil of Leschetizky in Vienna and was regarded as the best private music teacher in West Chester. He hosted recitals for his students and Barber attracted attention as a performer from the age of nine. Green was very particular about what his students played; he didn't like them all playing the same pieces; and he insisted on scale practice. Henry said that he had to work hard for his music but that it all came naturally to Sam.[31]

As a professional musician, Constant Vauclain was an informative, if dogmatic, witness. After Curtis, where he taught for twenty-five years, he joined the faculty at the University of Pennsylvania, from which he retired in 1979. Like Barber, he studied with Rosario Scalero at Curtis and provided details of his exacting demands:

> I went to Curtis because Sam advised me to. I know how he was taught. He was one of the very few superlatively taught composers in America in the twentieth century. . . . I had studied before with other teachers who were much too permissive and I decided to go through it all again and—on his advice—I went to his teacher Scalero. This was a matter of six years of working summer and winter and going through a long course in counterpoint in eight parts before we were allowed even to harmonize a chorale. This was all supposed to be done without touching a piano. . . . The only other composers in the twentieth century who had a course like this were Bartók, who studied the same way in Budapest, and Hindemith.[32]

---

31. Raymond Henry, interview with Brent D. Fegley, October 8, 1982.

32. Constant Vauclain (1908–2003), interview with Brent D. Fegley, January 8, 1982. Rosario Scalero (1870–1954), Italian violinist, composer, and teacher who studied in Italy, London, and Vienna. He was a pupil of the Austro-Hungarian musicologist and composer Eusebius Mandyczewski (1857–1929), a close friend of Brahms. In 1919 Scalero succeeded Ernest Bloch at the Mannes School of Music in New York and was on the faculty at Curtis from 1925 until he returned to Italy in 1946. He taught Barber at Curtis from 1925 to 1934 as well as in Italy. Barber has given a picture of life with Scalero in Italy—energetic walks in the mountains and, in spite of his academic bias, real enthusiasm for the popular singing group The Revellers. Heyman, *Samuel Barber: The Composer and His Music*, 55. But Scalero despaired of Barber's later style when he saw the Piano Sonata in 1951. Ibid., 310.

In a particularly lucid discussion, Vauclain confirmed that "the greatest early influence on Sam was his piano teacher, Green, his first teacher who was very helpful to him." He concluded by summing up Barber's overall position as he saw it in 1981:

> I think he was the most gifted composer on the American scene. His musical output was a reflection of the first half of the twentieth century rather than the second. . . . That was perfectly legitimate because that was what he was brought up in. . . . I think he found his own métier, his own kind of utterance. He was much too well-trained to get into the avant-garde, serialism or anything like that—for anybody with any real training this is just nonsense. It has clearly now become obvious. So he had the artistic integrity to pursue the idiom that was honestly his own in spite of the fact that he was criticized in some quarters . . . for being reactionary. Now a lot of other composers who were avant-garde have become even more reactionary than Sam—like Penderecki. This shows that perhaps he was ahead of the times instead of behind.[33]

Vauclain remembered that Barber said he kept a sheet of paper by his bed in case he thought of something in the middle of the night and did not want to forget it.

Barber himself admitted in interviews in this book, "I was very lucky always."[34] It was incredibly fortunate that the Curtis Institute was opened in nearby Philadelphia in 1924. The school was founded by Mary Louise Curtis Bok (1876–1970), whose father was the publishing magnate Cyrus Curtis. Before her father died in 1930, she had endowed the Curtis Institute with $12.5 million, which has enabled it to take all its students without charging fees ever since. Mary Bok attracted an outstanding faculty, and she provided for the Institute what today would be regarded as an imposing mission statement:

> It is my aim that earnest students shall acquire a thorough musical education, not learning only to sing or play, but also the history of music, the laws of its making, languages, ear-training and music appreciation.
>
> They shall learn to think and to express their thoughts against a background of quiet culture, with the stimulus of personal contact with artist-teachers who represent the highest and finest in their art.
>
> The aim is for quality of the work, rather than quick showy results.[35]

---

33. Vauclain, interview with Fegley. Krzysztof Penderecki (1933–), Polish composer who started as an avant-gardist with works such as *Threnody to the Victims of Hiroshima* (1960) and later moved back to traditional idioms.

34. See interview with Robert Sherman, chapter 4.

35. Heyman, *Samuel Barber: The Composer and His Music,* 33–34.

This fit Barber exactly as he proceeded to major in piano, voice, and composition and also to study languages. Further, he gathered awards that commended him to Mary Bok. These included the Bearns Prize, which he won in 1929 and again in 1933, the year he left Curtis; in 1935 he was awarded both the Prix de Rome and a Pulitzer Travel Scholarship. According to Bill and Marie Brosius, Mary Bok had given Barber his first car as well as a grand piano.[36] She paid for the early publications at G. Schirmer, probably unknown to Barber, and she helped with the purchase and extension of Capricorn, the house Barber and Menotti shared at Mt. Kisco outside New York from 1943 to 1973.

Barber went to Curtis in 1924, and Gian Carlo Menotti arrived from Italy four years later. The promising young Italian, who could barely speak English, was routed to Barber so they could talk in French. They immediately became friends—the rest is history—and their personal and professional partnership is documented in the interview with Menotti in this book (chapter 6).[37] Gian Carlo's father had died, and his mother had remarried and gone to live in South America after being advised by Toscanini to send her son to the Curtis Institute.

The two gifted students sometimes behaved badly. Menotti remembered:

> At a concert we were almost thrown out of the school because there was a soprano who was teaching voice who didn't have much voice left, but the faculty had to give a concert every year. At every recital she sang "Depuis le jour" from Charpentier's *Louise*. We were so bored that I made a bet with Sam: "Would you have the courage to drop a whole handful of coins when she hits the high note?" So he did—on a wooden floor. . . . We never realized that the money would not just stop—the coins kept going clink, clink, clink . . . all over the floor. We were lectured very severely![38]

On his own in America, Menotti was adopted by the Barber family. Once again, Barber was fortunate in being introduced to Italy through Menotti and his family. This provided a gateway to Europe and affected his life and his work. Menotti used to travel from New York, where he was living, to visit the Barbers even when Barber was at the American Academy in Rome:

> Then Sam wrote to me that he had gotten permission from the Academy to come back to the United States for a visit. We hadn't seen Sam for almost a year. He said he wanted to surprise his family, so he told them he was having his portrait painted by an Italian painter and told me: "Now you go and get a

---

36. Broder reported that his parents gave Sam a car on his sixteenth birthday, but he was so keen on walking that after he learned to drive he left it the garage. Broder, *Samuel Barber,* 11.

37. See also John Gruen, *Menotti: A Biography* (New York: Macmillan, 1978).

38. Menotti, interview with Brent D. Fegley, December 9, 1981.

huge frame and cover it: that's the portrait." Then I called Dr. and Mrs. Barber to tell them Sam's portrait had arrived. They were dying to see it so I brought this empty frame to West Chester and said: "Now you all get out of the room because I want to unveil it." Then Sam sneaked into the house and sat inside the frame. Then I unveiled the thing and there was Sam who said: "Hello!" Poor Mrs. Barber almost fainted![39]

All along, Barber benefited from his connections with the highest echelons of the musical world, but not only from Curtis: some were also members of his family. His aunt Louise Homer was married to the composer Sidney Homer, who acted as a remarkably perceptive adviser until his death in 1953. Barber had a high opinion of his uncle's songs and edited a collection of them that was published by Schirmer in 1943. His preface reveals something of his own inclinations, starting with the context: "With the present over-emphasis on orchestral music, much re-evaluation of American composers is apt to neglect the songwriter. Many a thick and mediocre orchestral score is carefully weighed, almost by the pound, and squeezed dry to find something of value, while excellent songs are totally ignored."[40]

Then Barber introduced his uncle, whose role in supporting his wife Louise's career was crucial:

Born in 1864 in Boston, Sidney Homer studied with Chadwick and later with Rheinberger in Munich.[41] Throughout his life, a sturdy New England self-reliance balanced his respect for European tradition. These two characteristics, successfully blended, have produced his best songs. By maintaining such an equilibrium he avoided the fate of some of his talented contemporaries, who tipped the scales too far to one side or the other and became either provincial amateurs, with a tang that often becomes too salty, or eclectics far too sensitive to the latest musical fashions from abroad.

In 1895, Mr. Homer married Louise Beatty, whose subsequent career at the Metropolitan is familiar to everyone. . . . It is not often, perhaps, that a composer has the privilege of pointing out the merits of his uncle's songs. From childhood on, at Lake George and New York, I have heard Mrs. Homer sing these songs.[42] She always used a group of them at every concert, and she did not give them a place only at the end of her programs, which is the common

---

39. Ibid.

40. Sidney Homer, *Seventeen Songs,* compiled with a preface by Samuel Barber (New York: G. Schirmer, 1943), 3.

41. George Whitefield Chadwick (1854–1931), New England composer and influential teacher. Josef Rheinberger (1839–1901), German organist, composer, and teacher whose American pupils included Chadwick and Horatio Parker.

42. The Homers had a house at Lake George, below the Adirondack Mountains in northern New York State, where Barber was a regular visitor.

destiny of most American songs, like after-dinner mints, for an audience whose best attention has been given elsewhere.[43]

Thus Barber repaid some of his debt to Homer, and, of course, his aunt regularly sang Barber's songs from his teens onward. A neighbor who knew the family well once asked Barber why he hadn't continued to cultivate his voice. He replied, "Because, when I talked to my uncle Sidney Homer, he said that composing is what I should do."[44] Barber admitted that he had considered "a serious career in singing as well as composition. . . . However, in order to be a good singer, you must be either extremely intelligent or extremely stupid, and as I didn't fit into either of these categories, I became a composer instead."[45]

Several friends of the Barber family whom Fegley interviewed found Barber's music beyond them—apparently including his mother—or considered it melancholy. Some remembered the Alma Mater he wrote for his high school and found it more palatable than anything that came later. But it was generally accepted that Barber's parents were proud of his achievements and that he was devoted to them. According to Frances T. Herron, one of Dr. Barber's patients, "I don't think they ever realized that he would become as famous as he did, but they were behind him because they were intelligent people that didn't try to make something of their son that wasn't there. . . . It was his aunt who really pushed him into this when she saw his potential."[46] But Dorothy Bates, a Henderson High School secretary who had been two years behind Barber in school, remembered his father saying that he felt Sam would "ask nothing more out of life than to starve in a garret and be a musician!"[47] So, although he may have been widely recognized as a genius, the acclaim Barber's subsequent career garnered was a surprise. His close friend Gian Carlo Menotti also became widely known. People in West Chester enjoyed meeting him.

Only one of the people interviewed by Fegley came close to mentioning Barber's sexuality. For the older people in West Chester, such things were not on the agenda for discussion, even in 1981. Larry Hickman, a high school contemporary, referred to the fact that he and Barber were in dancing class together and said that Barber was brilliant, well liked, and that his whole life was music. He then added: "But of course—you don't have to put this on tape—he was different." When the discussion came back to this topic later, the "difference" was protectively defined as an obsession with music.[48]

---

43. Homer, *Seventeen Songs*, 3.
44. Dean, interview with Fegley.
45. Coleman, "The Composer Talks with Emily Coleman," 69.
46. Frances T. Herron, interview with Brent D. Fegley, November 24, 1981.
47. Cited in Neary, "Samuel Barber: An Oral Recollection," 26.
48. Hickman, interview with Fegley, January 19, 1981.

Marie Brosius, who knew Sam from childhood on, reported on his personality and social activities: "I know one time he belonged to the Boy Scouts. . . . I have a photograph of him in the Boy Scouts up in the Poconos.[49] . . . Sam didn't socialize very much. A lot of people held that against him . . . and used to say he was stuck up. But it wasn't that, he was just shy. . . . He was afraid to commit himself to anything it seemed. But when you'd get talking to him it was all right. . . . He just couldn't start something with you and talk. . . . He was melancholy—all you have to do is look at his pictures! He was very deep . . . and worried about everything."[50]

Several people had the impression that Barber turned against West Chester; others pointed out that he was nevertheless buried there. John Sepalla, who was music director of the West Chester Area School District for thirty-eight years and always found Barber's music challenging, summed up: "The mere fact that Sam wanted to go back to his old church and be buried in West Chester proves he wasn't a stuck-up individual. He knew where his roots were and wanted to be there. After the funeral you had a very distinct impression of a great genius."[51] Menotti understood: "He loved Europe but also had a very soft spot for West Chester. He didn't like his life there very much—a small town. Well, what can you do in West Chester?"[52]

The relationship between Americans and Europe in the late nineteenth century is a major theme in the novels of Henry James. In *Roderick Hudson*, Rowland Mallett takes his protégé to Rome to develop as a sculptor: "[T]he old imperial city really delighted him; only there he found what he had been looking for from the first—the complete contradiction of Northampton."[53] In 1928, from the boat, Barber wrote home in identical terms: "I sit on the forward deck at the very bow of the boat looking towards Europe—as far as possible from West Chester as it is [in] my power to be!"[54] The difference was that James's hero was a failure and Barber became a success.

Robert Gawthrop understood: "When you are a composer you don't have too many people . . . who move in your circles. He came back to West Chester with some regularity but his interests kept him elsewhere. If I happened to be a mountaineer I'd go where the mountains are. But he did not have a dislike for West Chester."[55]

---

49. According to Barber's aunt, Ada Strode, the house in the Poconos belonged to Mrs. Scott, a neighbor in West Chester, "who had a studio built to the rear of the property where Sam did composing and studying during the summer." Strode, interview with Brent D. Fegley, October 31, 1981.

50. Marie Brosius, interview with Fegley.

51. Cited in Neary, "Samuel Barber: An Oral Recollection," 30.

52. Menotti, interview with Fegley.

53. Henry James, *Roderick Hudson* (London: Penguin, 1969 [1874]), 79.

54. Cited in Broder, *Samuel Barber*, 18. See Heyman, 53.

55. Gawthrop, interview with Fegley.

Barber's career could never have developed from a base in such a small town where he might have been expected to settle down with a daughter of a prominent family such as his own. It was no place for a young man with a gay lifestyle once it became clear that he and Gian Carlo were rather more than just boys together. Some people recalled seeing Sam with girls, but Bill and Marie Brosius thought there were no girlfriends: "He had a one-track mind—music and that was it. Nothing dared interfere with it."[56]

---

56. Bill and Marie Brosius, interviews with Fegley.

Chapter Two

Reception in England

PETER DICKINSON

The prolific American writer David Ewen, writing for a British public in the *Musical Times* in 1939, found Roy Harris "the most significant" among American composers but continued: "Samuel Barber promises to become the most important discovery since Harris."[1] Ewen heard Barber's First Symphony at the Salzburg Festival in 1937 where it was followed by an ovation. He went on prophetically in terms rarely used by any British writer then or later: "Samuel Barber's facility in self-expression, his extraordinary gift in formulating his copious ideas into a coherent and integrated pattern . . . his capacity for writing a line of melody, and his instinct for harmony and orchestration bespeak a formidable creative talent. . . . Samuel Barber is already a fine and original composer: there is every reason to believe he may ultimately develop into a great one."[2]

Harris has not stood the test of time, but the adulation accorded to Barber in America came early and was sustained, apart from a reaction that became perceptible in the 1960s. By looking at Barber's exposure in London, we see how his music gradually made its way in a major cultural capital outside the United States without the assumptions of genius common on its home ground.

The first hearing of his music in London was with a group of young musicians from the Curtis Institute, including the Curtis Quartet, sponsored by the Philadelphia branch of the English-Speaking Union in June 1935. They gave three concerts of American music, the first at Lady Astor's house in St. James's Square that included the Serenade, op. 1, for string quartet, *Dover Beach,* and four other songs.[3] Barber told his parents: "Lady Astor went behind the scenes during the

---

1. Roy Harris (1898–1981), prominent and prolific mid-twentieth-century American composer whose Third Symphony (1938) became widely known and admired.

2. David Ewen, "Modern American Composers," *Musical Times* (June 1939): 413–16.

3. Heyman, *Samuel Barber: The Composer and His Music,* 123. Nancy Witcher Astor, Viscountess Astor (1879–1964), the American-born Nancy Langhorne, moved to England in 1905 where she exercised influence as a rare female Member of Parliament (1919–45) and a prominent hostess to the elite at her husband's estate at Cliveden. She was a Christian Scientist and her interests included the group called Milner's Kindergarten, dedicated to supporting the unity of English-speaking peoples.

concert and complimented my music by asking if I was dead yet!"[4] The next time Barber's music was heard in London seems to have been when the Curtis Quartet played the Serenade at the Aeolian Hall on November 25, 1936. *The Times* merely referred to "a rhapsodical serenade by Samuel Barber and . . . Turina's *La Oracion del torero*—neither of them a work of great moment."[5] The following year Felix Salmond included Barber's Cello Sonata in his Wigmore Hall recital on June 21 with the composer at the piano; this performance was announced in *The Times* but may not have been reviewed.

More significant was the British premiere of the String Quartet given by the Curtis Quartet at the Aeolian Hall in November. As *The Times* reported: "It has a fine slow movement, a meditation that unfolds itself in spirals. Most composers find it easier to write quick movements than slow but Mr. Barber achieves a greater success with the more difficult task."[6] Indeed he did.

In June 1938 the festival of the International Society for Contemporary Music was held in London. Copland was represented by *El Salon Mexico*. There was nothing by Barber in the official program—there never would be—but Boosey and Hawkes put on a recital in its studio that included *Dover Beach* sung by Victor Harding with the Cardiff Ensemble. According to *The Times*, "This was not modern in the sense that the other works (Lennox Berkeley and Alan Bush) were, for it matched the nineteenth-century words very happily, but it did not sound outmoded and rang true."[7] As it happens, Vaughan Williams lectured at Bryn Mawr College in 1932, met Barber, and heard him sing *Dover Beach* to his own accompaniment. According to Barber, Vaughan Williams congratulated him and said: "I tried several times to set *Dover Beach* but you really *got* it!"[8]

---

4. Cited in Broder, *Samuel Barber,* 29.

5. "Recitals of the Week," *The Times,* November 27, 1936. Reviews in this newspaper are unsigned. References can be reached at *The Times* Digital Archive 1785–1985 (archive. timesonline.co.uk/tol/archive).

6. "Weekend Concerts," *The Times,* November 8, 1937.

7. "Contemporary Music Festival," *The Times,* June 24, 1938. Sir Lennox Berkeley (1903–89); Alan Bush (1900–1995).

8. Quoted in Heyman, *Samuel Barber: The Composer and His Music,* 94. Vaughan Williams gave the Fifth Series of Mary Flexner Lectures in the Humanities at Bryn Mawr College and was there from about October 21 to November 1. He was impressed in various ways: "I went to a supper party where we all sat round (about fifty) and sang Brahms' Requiem—not at all bad." Their rich lawyer host was "violently keen on Brahms." And: "I had to stand up before a class the day after each lecture and be heckled by a crowd of young women who asked 'what I meant by' then they referred to their note books—I've come off fairly unscathed up to the present." Letter to Diana Audrey, October 24, 1932, in Hugh Cobbe, ed., *Letters of Ralph Vaughan Williams 1895–1958* (Oxford: Oxford University Press, 2008), 205. The lectures were published as *National Music* (Oxford: Oxford University Press, 1934).

Barber's *First Essay* was given at the Proms on August 24, 1939. *The Times* reported: "This short and simple piece is well constructed from not very appealing material. . . . [T]hough it does not suggest a composer of outstanding originality, it avoids triteness and false brilliance. The points are well made by a practised hand."[9]

Then there were wartime concerts on which Barber's music continued to appear prominently with a positive response. What was announced as the British premiere of the First Symphony took place at an Anglo-American Promenade concert on August 5, 1941: "[I]f the final drawing of conclusions involves some pretty drastic counterpoint there is no doubt about its intelligibility, cohesion and cogency."[10] In the same year: "Samuel Barber's *Essay for Orchestra* deserves to be better known on this side of the Atlantic. It is too short to create a sensation but not to show the skill of the composer in mixing colors or to be thoroughly enjoyed."[11]

The famous National Gallery recitals that continued throughout the war in spite of the danger from bombing announced a program of American music for March 9, 1942: "The American label on a concert of the National Gallery type is a little formidable. People do not know what they are in for." In fact, Astra Desmond sang some songs and Norina Semino and Harry Isaacs played the Cello Sonata, dedicated to Barber's teacher Scalero, which "deserves to be better known. . . . [It is] thoughtful and attractive in thematic material and would take its place fitly in any mixed program of today's music."[12] The sonata continued to be played regularly.

Barber had another work in the Proms on June 23, 1944—the British premiere of the Violin Concerto. By now *The Times* could say: "Barber's name is already familiar in this country . . . his music has been widely played throughout Europe and the Americas" and continued: "beneath his external reticence of expression, it is immediately apparent that the music was born of deep feeling." But the reviewer concluded that the third movement is actually a scherzo that ought to be followed by a real finale—"an emotional climax such as the composer is obviously capable of producing and the listener instinctively seeks."[13]

---

9. "Promenade Concert," *The Times*, August 25, 1939.

10. "Promenade Concert: An Anglo-American Programme," *The Times*, August 5, 1941. But see Heyman, *Samuel Barber: The Composer and His Music*, 144, where she cites a London performance under Rodzinsky on June 24, 1937.

11. Unsigned, "New Music," *Musical Times* (December 1941): 430.

12. "National Gallery Concerts," *The Times*, March 11, 1942.

13. "A Violin Concerto from America," *The Times*, June 26, 1944. The question of balancing the movements within the concerto raises an important issue about the tempo of the first movement. In John Ardoin, "Samuel Barber at Capricorn," *Musical America* (March 1960): 4, 5, 46, the composer discussed recordings of his music and said: "I wish there might be a good version of my Violin Concerto in which the first movement is

On March 20, 1945, the National Symphony Orchestra under Sidney Beer gave the British premiere of *School for Scandal Overture* at the Royal Albert Hall. The following season the unrivalled film composer Bernard Herrmann conducted it with the Hallé Orchestra, and it appeared again in an American Music Prom with the London Symphony Orchestra under Basil Cameron in 1956: "in the main stream of European music, a well-shaped piece of expert craftsmanship, its wit nicely poised, its lyricism warm." The reviewer continued with a vicious attack on Gershwin's Piano Concerto.[14]

On June 21, 1945, the Blech Quartet played Barber's Quartet at the Contemporary Music Centre. *The Times* reported: "Barber's quartet contains a good slow movement which recalls the methods and something of the feeling of later Vaughan Williams. It is approachable music, with some distinctive character confirming the entry of America into the international field of chamber music."[15] Five days later the Blech Quartet played the Quartet again at the Wigmore Hall; press announcements wrongly claimed it as the British premiere.

By that time the Toscanini[16] recording of the *Adagio for Strings* had come out, and *Gramophone* declared: "Barber has an eloquence that I like: he lets himself go, and finds a richness of string speech that will be cordially enjoyed. It is shapely, well-knit music, conservative in idiom, expressive, dignified; music of a good brain that . . . also makes one believe in the composer's heart."[17] The recording also impressed William McNaught: "This work has come to the front for good reason. . . . [I]t holds the attention by steady growth and plan: not many

---

not taken too slowly." When I corresponded with Annette Kaufman, the widow of Louis Kaufman, who made the first recording of the Violin Concerto in 1953 (Concert Hall CHE-8, followed by various reissues, then Orion LP ORS-79355 in 1980), she explained that Koussevitzky, who conducted an early performance with Ruth Posselt, was notorious for his slow tempi (letters to me of April 28 and May 10, 2001). "Barber discussed carefully that he would prefer a livelier tempo for the first movement than what Maestro Koussevitzky directed." However, Kaufman was still below the metronome mark. Barbara Heyman summed up: "I have checked his personal copy of the score—the one he conducted from and which has some notations to himself—and there is no indication that he intended the tempo of the first movement to be taken any slower than marked (quarter-note = 100). . . . [T]he only way the last movement can be regarded as an integrated part of the whole concerto . . . is if the first movement is played as a true *allegro*, as indicated in the score. That way the two outer movements are balanced." Heyman, e-mail to me, September 12, 2001. Is it too late to right this wrong?

14. "American Music Prom," *The Times*, August 27, 1956.

15. "Contemporary Music Centre," *The Times*, June 22, 1945.

16. Arturo Toscanini (1867–1957), Italian conductor with an outstanding international reputation who settled in New York where the NBC Orchestra was created for him in 1937. He launched Barber's *Adagio* on November 5, 1938.

17. *Adagio*, NBC Symphony Orchestra/Toscanini, HMV DB 6180; Review, *Gramophone* (February 1945): 15. All *Gramophone* reviews are at www.gramophone.net.

composers put such faith in sustained equable strength and reposeful movement. . . . [O]ne returns again and again to this griefless elegy to observe how much meaning can be patiently drawn from a slow, conjunct diatonic melody in contrast to the garrulous haste and bustling figures that are the fashion."[18]

In 1945 the *Adagio for Strings* was in the Proms on August 5; it was also played by the New London Orchestra under Anatole Fistoulari at the Cambridge Theatre on September 16 and by the New London Orchestra under Alec Sherman on December 15, 1946. Now the *Adagio* was firmly established in England and would soon go further.

In 1946 Barber conducted it at the Three Choirs Festival with the London Symphony Orchestra in Hereford Cathedral in a very British context, with works by George Dyson, Charles Wood, and Vaughan Williams performed the same day.[19] This was the territory so successfully invaded by an earlier American composer, Horatio Parker, when his oratorio *Hora Novissima* was performed at the Three Choirs in 1899; a commission followed, and he was admired by Elgar. On that same visit Barber conducted a program of his own works with the BBC Northern Orchestra, broadcast on September 24 on the BBC Home Service. On January 16, 1947, the Jacques Orchestra gave the "now well-known *Adagio*" at the Wigmore Hall,[20] and in 1955 it was included in the Prize Day concert at the Royal College of Music in the presence of the Queen Mother.[21] But by 1950 Barber was paying for the preeminence of the *Adagio*, as Lionel Salter indicated when reviewing the Boyd Neel Orchestra's recording, which he found much too fast: "As far as the British public is concerned, Samuel Barber is for all practical purposes the composer of this charming *Adagio* and nothing else."[22] Over half a century later, after the 9/11 atrocities, Leonard Slatkin inserted the *Adagio* into the Last Night of the Proms at the Royal Albert Hall, with the BBC Symphony Orchestra, on September 15, 2001.

On October 7, 1946, Sidney Harrison included the *Four Excursions* in his Wigmore Hall piano recital. The popular styles that Barber represented in his own way drew this response and put Barber above all his colleagues: "Samuel Barber who is beginning to appear as America's most considerable composer with something distinctively American to say, certainly writes American music in

---

18. William McNaught, "Gramophone Notes," *Musical Times* (May 1945): 149. But in 1948, when he also knew the first two *Essays* and the Cello Sonata, McNaught responded in lukewarm fashion to the First Symphony. McNaught, "Gramophone Notes," *Musical Times* (October 1948): 304.

19. "Three Choirs Festival: English Secular Music," *The Times*, September 13, 1946.

20. "Weekend Concerts," *The Times,* January 19, 1947.

21. "Prize Day at RCM," *The Times*, November 4, 1955.

22. Lionel Salter, Review: Decca X305, *Gramophone* (June 1950): 14.

Excursions."[23] On December 16, 1946, the Boyd Neel Orchestra gave the British premiere of the Serenade, op. 1, in its orchestral version.[24]

On November 24, 1948, Amaryllis Fleming played the Cello Sonata at the Wigmore Hall.[25] In August 1950 it was played at the Edinburgh Festival and could be heard twice in one week in London in November—and it has never looked back.

In 1949 the lead article in the periodical *Musical Opinion* acclaimed Barber and American music in general:

> The work of American composers is becoming increasingly familiar to listeners in this country . . . because the importance of many American compositions demands that they must be heard wherever the finest contemporary music is valued. Samuel Barber is the one most likely to appeal to English ears. His work is remarkable chiefly for its design, for its emotional stability, its controlled enthusiasm, its depth of feeling, which scorns obvious expression or over-elaborated detail; its bigness of thought and its humanity. . . . Of his importance no student of his work can long remain in doubt. His serious approach to the art of music, his prodigious technique, his record of work and achievement, not only command our profound respect but lead us to expect even greater things.[26]

The status of the Piano Sonata, which Barbara Heyman has called a "monumental masterpiece of its time,"[27] was not immediately clear in London after the American pianist Robert Wallenborn gave the British premiere at the Wigmore Hall on November 17, 1950. The reviewer surprisingly found the slow movement to be "mostly pianistic padding," but otherwise the work was "original and attractive." The writing was "hard and spare, with no unnecessary doubling and thickening of texture." The finale had to be repeated.[28] *The Times* damned the work with faint praise: "an efficient essay in pianistic thinking with a deft scherzo and stimulating fugal finale."[29] The first BBC broadcast of the Piano Sonata was given by Moura Lympany on December 7, 1950; Barber was in England and heard the broadcast.

---

23. "Wigmore Hall," *The Times*, October 9, 1946. The American pianist Alfred Popper also played the *Excursions* in his Wigmore Hall recital on June 21, 1947, as did Joan Moore on June 2, 1958.

24. "Boyd Neel Orchestra," *The Times*, December 16, 1946.

25. "Recitals of the Week," *The Times*, November 29, 1948.

26. Harold Dexter, "Samuel Barber and His Music," *Musical Opinion* 858 (March 1949): 285–86; 859 (April 1949): 343–44.

27. B. Heyman, *Samuel Barber: The Composer and His Music*, 308.

28. "London Music," *Musical Times* (December 1950): 482.

29. "Recitals of the Week," *The Times*, November 20, 1950.

The work soon became a repertory piece in subsequent Wigmore Hall recitals—notably when Natasha Litvin, Stephen Spender's wife, played it from memory at her Wigmore Hall recital on January 17, 1951.[30] Regular performances followed, with Bela Siki in 1951: "a good modern sonata for the piano"; Thomas Brockman in 1953; Marjorie Mitchell in 1954; Robert Goldsand: "solid musical worth . . . seems to be the most popular modern piano sonata," in 1954 and again in 1960; Patricia Carroll in 1955; Shura Cherkassky in 1957; Daphne Spottiswoode in 1958: "not very remarkable for its invention but expertly conceived for the medium"; Marjorie Mitchell again in 1959; Leslie Riskowitz in 1959; Mack Jost in 1959; Leslie Atkinson in 1960, reviewed as "[p]ianist with the wrong program"; Clifton Matthews in 1960; Robert Guralnik in 1961; John Covelli: "well-knit composition"; and Thomas Mastroianni in 1964: "Philadelphian excels in Samuel Barber's fine Piano Sonata . . . the final fugue a really exciting climax to the recital."[31] The connection with Horowitz, who gave the premiere and twenty further performances that first season, must have challenged many pianists who have taken to the sonata like a young actor straining at the leash to play his first Hamlet—and these are only some of the London performances.[32] As early as 1952, Hans Tischler regarded the "fusion of contemporary technique with that of the past three centuries" as having created "a classic of our times."[33] Of particular importance was the recital given by John Browning at the Wigmore Hall on January 29, 1962. Barber wrote his Piano Concerto for Browning, which would be premiered in the new Philharmonic Hall in New York City in September and first heard in London on January 8, 1963. *The Times* review of Browning's Wigmore recital was headed "An Outstanding Pianist" and continued: "Schumann's *Symphonic Studies* and Samuel Barber's Sonata are virtuoso pieces; Mr. Browning completely transcended their technical difficulties and presented them with all the rhetoric, poetry and musical logic one could ask for. This was great playing."[34]

---

30. "Recitals of the Week," *The Times,* January 22, 1951. Barber was a friend of the poet and critic Stephen Spender (1909–95) and set his poem in *A Stopwatch and an Ordinance Map,* op. 15, for male voices and timpani in 1940. Barber conducted the premiere with the Madrigal Chorus he ran at Curtis during the years 1939–41.

31. *The Times,* March 6, 1951; October 26, 1953; March 22, 1954; November 8, 1954; October 10, 1955; March 4, 1957; November 17, 1958; May 4, 1959; May 22, 1959; December 15, 1959; February 25, 1960; September 22, 1960; December 22, 1960; October 21, 1961; September 17 and 19, 1964. Recordings have included Horowitz (1950), Mitchell (1967), Guralnik (1970), and Browning (1971).

32. Vladimir Horowitz (1903–89), Russian-born American pianist. "One of the supreme pianists in history": Harold C. Schonberg, *The New Grove Dictionary of Music and Musicians,* 2nd ed., ed. Stanley Sadie (London: Macmillan, 2001), vol. 11, 739–40.

33. Hans Tischler, "Barber's Piano Sonata, Op 26," *Music and Letters* (October 1952): 352–54.

34. *The Times,* January 30, 1962.

In 1950 Norman Demuth, composer, teacher, and authority on French music, wrote a book entitled *Musical Trends in the Twentieth Century* in which he showed unusual understanding of Barber's position compared with what was to follow in Britain and the United States: "Barber is drawn to the romantic virtuosity of Strauss as viewed through late twentieth-century eyes. . . . It might be said that he is a reactionary, until it is realized that he deliberately withholds himself from the trend of neo-classicism." Demuth goes on to identify the Italian influence, suggests a counterpart in Respighi, and recognizes the *Adagio* as a standard work.[35] He regards the First Symphony as "a noble work of its kind even if it is not very new" but rates it below Roy Harris's Third. He finds Barber's music "a connecting link between the old and the new," with its "skilful avoidance of too highly charged emotion masterly and natural." Demuth sums up: "It is refreshing to meet this unashamed romanticism today, and one hopes that Barber will have a little influence upon the young idea in this regard."[36] Not yet, however.

George Weldon, conducting the City of Birmingham Symphony Orchestra, took up Barber's First Symphony. He conducted it at Wolverhampton in 1949 and again at the Royal Festival Hall in 1951, wrongly presumed to have been the belated first London hearing. Both performances were favorably reviewed. Of the latter *The Times* said: "This is a powerful cri-de-coeur. . . . [I]ts language, indebted like its structure to Sibelius, yet has the force of a personality which acknowledges no apron-strings."[37]

In 1951, Edward Sackville-West summed up Barber's British profile:

I do not find the Second Symphony of this fertile and gifted composer as successful as the lovely 'Cello Concerto, or as the Medea ballet, to which it is materially akin. This is only a comparative judgment: all three works are superior examples of a modern style that, while remaining true to its own laws of harmonic development, can without difficulty be understood and enjoyed even by listeners whose taste does not incline towards contemporary music in general. Samuel Barber's works are, I believe, widely popular in America and could easily become so here, for his melodic gift is very winning, his rhythmic sense lively, and his forms are clear and strong. With Aaron Copland he seems to me the most talented practitioner of what has now become recognisable as a distinctively American style in music.[38]

---

35. Ottorino Respighi (1876–1936), Italian composer of pictorial orchestral extravaganzas such as *The Fountains of Rome* (1916).

36. Norman Demuth, *Musical Trends in the Twentieth Century* (London: Rockcliff, 1952), 317–18.

37. *The Times*, June 20, 1949; June 22, 1951.

38. Sackville-West, "A Quarterly Retrospect: April–June 1951," *Gramophone* (August 1951): 7.

The next London performance of the First Symphony with the BBC Symphony Orchestra under Sir Malcolm Sargent at the Royal Festival Hall on December 9, 1953, was also well received.[39] Then the work's career went further. The Ballet des Champs-Elysées presented *La damnée* in Paris with choreography by Walter Gore set to the First Symphony.[40] Two years later Gore's own company put on the ballet in London with the English title *The Crucifix*.[41] In 1958 Peter Wright's ballet *A Blue Rose* choreographed Barber's *Souvenirs* for the junior dancers of the Royal Ballet—"attractive neo-romantic dance music."[42]

In 1956 Barber's *Second Essay* was given its British premiere by the Royal Philharmonic Orchestra under Sir Adrian Boult. *The Times* reported: "decidedly interesting music with a vivid scherzo as its central section followed by an impressive slow movement built up to a noble climax."[43]

But opposition clouds had begun to gather. The Britten and Mahler scholar Donald Mitchell reacted dismissively to the first British performance of *Prayers of Kierkegaard* at the Royal Festival Hall on June 10, 1955: "Barber's settings are of substantial length, continuous in design and solemnly conceived. The music is always deft and fluent, but lacks pungency and bite; it leaves an impression of a creatively unmotivated display of excellent craftsmanship. If Barber has a style at all, it belongs to the category of contemporary academicism, a kind of tasteful middle-brow modernity that may have a topical function but will not prove of much interest to the future."[44]

This coincides with Virgil Thomson's assessment of Barber as "high middle-brow"; it may reflect the Anglo-American problem identified by John Browning in his interview in this book; and it could also be an example of what Thomson regarded as the Britten monopoly that Donald Mitchell was so instrumental in establishing.[45]

The Times critic heard *The Prayers of Kierkegaard* differently: "The choral writing is bold and the orchestral elaborate. There is a bite in it which accords with the Danish theologian's austere piety. . . . It had a certain stark impressiveness and sounds a new note in modern choral music."[46]

---

39. "Festival Hall: BBC Concert," *The Times*, December 10, 1953.

40. "English Ballets in Paris," *The Times*, November 8, 1951.

41. "Princes Theatre: Walter Gore Ballet," *The Times*, September 23, 1953.

42. "Covent Garden: Royal Ballet," *The Times*, December 27, 1957.

43. "Weekend Concerts: Royal Philharmonic Society," *The Times*, April 15, 1956.

44. Donald Mitchell, "London Music," *Musical Times* (August 1955): 433. See also Donald Mitchell and Hans Keller, eds., *Benjamin Britten: A Commentary on His Works from a Group of Specialists* (London: Rockcliff, 1952).

45. See interviews with John Browning (chapter 12) and Virgil Thomson (chapter 10).

46. "Kierkegaard Cantata: LPO at the Festival Hall," *The Times*, June 11, 1955.

For Mitchell the writing lacked the quality of "bite" *The Times* critic particularly identified. Barber was present at the concert, which he attended with Aaron Copland, who had been equally well represented on the London concert scene since before the war.

Two years later Harold Rutland, editor of the *Musical Times,* found *Medea's Meditation and Dance of Vengeance* to have both "power and craftsmanship."[47] *The Times* recognized a suitable subject for the Martha Graham ballet as "skilful and colorful music passing through Strauss's and Stravinsky's kind of reflection on Mediterranean antiquity . . . [but it] only just passes the test of viability on the concert platform and does not tell us much about Barber."[48]

Then *Vanessa* came on the scene. Robin Hull, in the *Musical Times,* reported that the opera had been acclaimed at the Met in 1958 and relayed from the Salzburg Festival on the BBC Third Program. Presumably relying on this radio broadcast, he reacted dismissively:

> Frankly, this work was a great disappointment. It was not merely that Menotti had provided a trashy libretto, on the lines of a penny novelette, but that the composer furnished a neo-Straussian score of quite superlative dullness. The irony of this misadventure lay in the fact that Barber showed an extraordinary technical skill in his handling of words. . . . He revealed, too, an enviable resource and sureness of touch in his contrivance of orchestral commentary, yet even this could not disguise the startling lack of individuality in the music itself.[49]

If this is a trashy libretto, there are plenty more in the operatic repertoire. However, worse was yet to come when Michael Markus reported: "There can be little doubt that the major talking point of this year's Salzburg Festival was *Vanessa.* Not because of its merits—it has none—but because it was an artistic catastrophe of the highest order."[50] In contrast, Raymond Ericson proclaimed: "If operas were ever designed to be sure-fire successes, *Vanessa* would fall in this category."[51] The review in *The Times* from Our Special Correspondent in New York was favorable and so, largely, was the report from Our Music Critic at the Salzburg production: "Mr. Barber's ideas are varied and exceedingly skilful. If the music is at times a little eclectic, it is always interesting and there are some very good tunes. Mr. Menotti's libretto is a good one."[52] Much later, reviewing a Trinity College of

---

47. Harold Rutland, "Thomas Schippers," *Musical Times* (March 1957): 157.

48. "Festival Hall: Celebrity Concert," *The Times,* February 1, 1957.

49. Robin Hull, "Broadcast Music," *Musical Times* (October 1958): 546.

50. Michael Marcus, "Successes and Failures at Salzburg," *Music and Musicians* (October 1958): 11.

51. Raymond Ericson, "*Vanessa*—the New Samuel Barber Opera," *Opera Annual* 5 (1958): 116.

52. "Mr. S. Barber's *Vanessa,*" *The Times,* January 17, 1958; "An Ibsenite Opera at Salzburg," *The Times,* August 18, 1958.

Music production of *Vanessa* at the Bloomsbury Theatre in London on July 8 and 9, 1999, Tim Ashley said: "A brave work—lyrical and compassionate, yet shot through with bitterness. . . . Its neglect by the major British opera companies remains shameful."[53]

The negative aspects of these sharply divided views anticipated the 1960s and showed what was coming.

On October 10, 1959, the New York Philharmonic's Royal Festival Hall concert under Leonard Bernstein included Barber's *Second Essay*. Harold Rutland found it a "neo-romantic piece with arabesque-like themes" that showed off the string section. Then he launched into an attack on Ives's *The Unanswered Question* that showed total incomprehension.[54] Barber, who disliked Ives, would have been sympathetic. *The Times* reported on the *Essay* as "a single movement of taut, sane and vigorous writing, academic in method, modern in feeling, unproblematic and acceptable." Again, *The Unanswered Question* would have been "terrible if it had not been so short."[55] Barber was again being stigmatized as academic, but that reaction to Ives would change. As Ives began to be regarded as a representative American composer, Barber would suffer.

As the 1960s progressed, the critical climate became more hostile toward both Barber and other traditionalists. *The Times* reviewed a recording of Barber's First and Harris's Third symphonies. Surprisingly, in view of Harris's iconic status in the United States, we read: "Barber's is the more immediately compelling. It is romantic, full of strong rhythms and themes and colorfully orchestrated, but though thrilling in part as a whole it does not satisfy. Barber is an eclectic composer. One is continually conscious of other musical influences—Shostakovich and Bartók for instance, but Barber does not emerge as a distinctive musical personality."[56] Presumably one is equally distracted by echoes of Stravinsky when listening to Copland or Tippett? Or by the impact of Haydn on Beethoven?

At this stage even Barber's songs—so widely admired—were misunderstood. The young Nicholas Maw[57] reviewed choral versions of some of the best-known songs: "For somebody as much esteemed as he, these should be better music. . . . 'Under the willow tree' is an attempt to pastiche an American folk song, the sort of thing that Copland does, and does much better. . . . In general the pieces are well enough written, everything is in place, all is as expected; but the flaccid

---

53. Ashley, "A Grand Performance: Samuel Barber's First Opera," *Guardian*, July 12, 1999. On November 15, 2003, BBC Radio 3 presented a semi-staged performance at the Barbican conducted by Leonard Slatkin.

54. Rutland, "New York Philharmonic," *Musical Times* (December 1959): 671.

55. "Like Burnished Copper: N. Y. Orchestra's Fine Tone," *The Times*, October 12, 1959.

56. "The Gramophone: From a Correspondent," *The Times*, October 8, 1960. Mercury MG 53007.

57. Nicholas Maw (1935–2009), prominent British composer who moved to the United States in 1984.

invention and the all-pervading atmosphere of staleness are insupportable, even by competent workmanship."[58]

The British premiere of Barber's Piano Concerto was relayed on BBC Radio 3 on January 9, 1963. In his review, Ronald Crichton enthused about Britten's "sublime *War Requiem*" and then compared the two composers:

> Both composers use a traditional tonal language, as the phrase is, but whereas Britten's music is fresh, personal and totally valid, Barber's sounds second-hand—a resourceful imitation, never the real thing. The concerto is a conventionally florid affair: ostentatiously lush and distressed in the first movement, wistful in the second and brassily emphatic in the third. The solo part, with its massive chords and scalic cascades, was clearly both difficult and enjoyable to play, and John Browning played it with stunning virtuosity.[59]

This level of incomprehension about one of Barber's finest works from an otherwise perceptive critic is difficult to explain except through Thomson's theory of the Britten monopoly here harnessed against Barber.[60] Perhaps British ears had become so accustomed to Britten's use of traditional materials that other composers tilling similar ground, even British ones, were at a disadvantage.

The detractors continued through the 1960s, with Wilfrid Mellers reviewing the Violin Concerto: "Barber's Concerto, in comparison [with Hindemith's on the same LP], is a dreadful piece, sloppy in its lyricism, self-indulgent in harmony and texture. Pretty pentatonic doodlings of the type associated with the lesser 'western' movie are inflated to symphonic proportions; far from being a masterpiece, the Concerto seems to me to do scant justice even to Barber's modest talent. Presumably [Isaac] Stern and [Leonard] Bernstein believe in it, for the performance seems better than could be expected."[61]

---

58. Nicholas Maw, "Choral," *Musical Times* (August 1961): 508.

59. Ronald Crichton, "London Music," *Musical Times* (March 1963): 192. Crichton relented somewhat when he reviewed the LP of Dietrich Fischer-Dieskau "at his incomparable best" singing *Dover Beach*—"its sincerity and high promise justify its inclusion here." CBS 72687; Crichton, "Record Reviews," *Musical Times* (February 1969): 165.

60. See interview with Virgil Thomson (chapter 10).

61. Wilfrid Mellers, "Gramophone Records," *Musical Times* (November 1965): 867. See also Mellers's *Music in a New Found Land* (London: Barrie and Rockcliff, 1964), 194–203, for Mellers's assessment of Barber where he admires the *Adagio* and finds *Knoxville: Summer of 1915* "honestly touching" but *Vanessa* "perversely nasty . . . a most unpleasant gloating over a woman's self-imprisonment, both physical and mental." See also Mellers, *Between Old Worlds and New* (London: Cygnus Arts, 1997), for his review of Heyman, *Samuel Barber: The Composer and His Music*, 247–49. Mellers's estimate of Barber was predictable, since more than two decades earlier he wrote: "The works we have heard of John Alden Carpenter, Deems Taylor, Ernest Schelling, Samuel Barber and the like may have been written down in America in the twentieth century; but they were born and bred in the drawing-rooms of nineteenth-century Europe and might well have stayed there." Mellers, "Language and Function in American Music," *Scrutiny* (April 1942): 346.

History has made mincemeat of that judgment—there were twenty-six record-ings current in 2008. In any case, it is a strange reaction coming after the pub-lication of Mellers's generous pioneering book on American music. Since he doesn't mention the three concertos, it looks as if he wrote his section on Bar-ber without considering them? As late as 1980 Mellers still considered Barber a "composer of adolescence."[62]

On September 19, 1972, there was another performance of Barber's *Second Essay*, this time from the Royal Philharmonic Orchestra at the Royal Festival Hall. Max Harrison, a normally balanced critic, reviewed the concert:

> Though his symphonies are the clearest demonstration of the fact, Samuel Barber's music usually becomes unsure of itself as it reaches beyond the expression of direct, simple, chiefly nostalgic feeling. True, the orchestral *Essay No. 2* gesticulates rather confidently in a rather conventional way, and is an improvement on No. 1 (which Toscanini used to play). But very little is actually said, and the rhetoric becomes unduly inflated towards the end. As might be expected of a conservative lyricist, Barber's trouble is that his two main themes are insufficiently contrasted to provide grit for a productive musical conflict. His orchestral colors are quite personal in the softer passages where the com-poser's still small voice can best be heard, and these give the piece an identity. Yet they grow muddy when the late, or belated, romantic gestures return, and Rudolph Kempe's noisily emphatic performance is probably the best answer to this emptiness.[63]

When I reviewed the original cast LP of *Vanessa* in 1978, I was becoming uncom-fortable about this kind of response to Barber:

> Barber's romantic music is often discussed with unnecessary cynicism. . . . But this old recording is a disappointment. Such latter-day Straussian sumptuous music needs a better recorded sound to emerge with any satisfaction. . . . The claims on the sleeve—"Barber's mastery of the operatic language . . . is second to none on the Salzburg-Milan axis" (Paul Henry Lang)—contrast strongly with Virgil Thomson in his book on American music: "standard Metropolitan operas, and no remarkable improvement on those of Deems Taylor or Howard Hanson." This followed immodest comment on Thomson's own operas, but nevertheless Thomson is right.[64]

---

62. Wilfrid Mellers, "Samuel Barber at Seventy," *Records and Recording* (July 1980): 31–32.

63. Harrison, "Music in London," *Musical Times* (November 1972): 1099.

64. Peter Dickinson, "Record Reviews," *Musical Times* (October 1978): 864; *Vanessa*, RCA Red Seal RL 02094–2; Virgil Thomson, *American Music since 1910* (London: Weiden-feld, and Nicolson, 1971).

Thirty years later I don't think Thomson was right. There's no comparison between the routine scoring of Hanson's *Merry Mount*, admittedly badly served by a 1933 recording, and the subtle atmospheric delineation in the orchestration of *Vanessa*.[65] Paul Griffiths, a modernist capable of being trenchant, was more balanced and perceptive than some of the British critics just quoted: "Samuel Barber occupies a place in American music comparable with that of Walton on this side of the Atlantic. Indeed if you imagine Walton's music with the traces of Prokofiev and Elgar replaced by echoes of Copland and Richard Strauss, then you have a fair idea of what to expect." Griffiths found the Violin Concerto "heady romantic stuff, securely tonal and everything a violin concerto should be" and admired *Knoxville: Summer of 1915* "because its nostalgic text justifies the luxuriant conservatism of the music."[66]

A concert was held in London to mark Barber's seventieth birthday, although he was not well enough to be present. This was given by the chief British new music group—the London Sinfonietta. They performed *Summer Music*, the String Quartet, the Serenade, *Dover Beach, Knoxville: Summer of 1915*, and some songs.[67]

In 1981 I wrote a brief obituary citing Barber as "one of the most widely performed American composers of this century, possibly because his music fits easily into the international mainstream of the early twentieth century. . . . Barber achieved this status in an environment which has been increasingly unfavorable to expressive romanticism, and he consistently held to his own path."[68]

The Times headed its obituary "Leading American Composer" and went on: "Barber enjoyed steady popularity as a composer of a wide range of works. . . . His temperament tended towards the romantic and the lyrical rather than the neo-classical and the many experimental trends on modern composition largely passed him by. His early works indeed tended to sound conservative but he was always an expressive composer who developed a highly individual style: and his reputation held steady, even tended to increase, as the years went by."[69]

"A highly individual style"—the very quality he had been accused of lacking by others.

---

65. Howard Hanson (1896–1981), *Merry Mount*, op. 31, original cast recording, Naxos 8–110024/5.

66. Paul Griffiths, "Record Reviews," *Musical Times* (October 1978): 864. See interviews with Thomson (chapter 10) and Copland (chapter 8) for further comparison between Barber and Walton.

67. Noel Goodwin, "Samuel Barber: Spitalfields," *The Times*, July 7, 1980. Goodwin lamented that the *Hermit Songs* and *Knoxville* were better known "in memorable choreography by Alvin Ailey than as concert works." Alvin Ailey (1931–89), founder of the Alvin Ailey American Dance Theater, who created seventy-nine ballets.

68. Peter Dickinson, "Obituary: Samuel Barber," *Musical Times* (March 1981): 193.

69. "Obituary: Mr. Samuel Barber," *The Times*, January 26, 1981.

The only work by Barber performed at the Aldeburgh Festivals during Benjamin Britten's lifetime was the *Hermit Songs* in 1968, but Barber's seventy-fifth anniversary in 1985 was marked with *Knoxville: Summer of 1915* and two songs.[70]

This investigation into British responses to Barber has revealed several stages. First, the idea of an American composer outside the popular field was unfamiliar. In 1974, when I started the Music Department at Keele University, I told a senior member of the university's governing body that we would be having a program in American music. He said: "American music? Is there any?" Further, the golden start that Barber's career had from his Curtis Institute days onward, with a plethora of prizes and awards, had conditioned the American musical public to expect great things from a composer with a conservative style who could make contact with audiences. He delivered the goods, but the advantage of knowing this background was less available in Britain. However, as soon as it became clear that Barber had a solid command of his craft, he gained recognition regardless of being an American. Further, coming from the country that was Britain's principal ally in World War II must have stood him in good stead in London, as the reception of these performances has shown.

After World War II, as we have seen, younger British critics came on the scene and, certainly as the 1960s approached, they became more committed to mainstream modernism and the continental avant-garde. The situation became polarized, so composers with a public were treated with suspicion. Boulez refused to serve on a panel organized by Hans Keller because Britten was included; Luigi Nono wouldn't shake hands with Britten at the Dartington Summer School in the late 1950s.[71] This climate told against Barber, too, whose nearest British counterpart, William Walton, was also regarded as repeating himself in an outmoded idiom through his later work.

This saga has a happy ending: Barber has been vindicated. All that is needed is a glance at the current record catalog where the figures for the number of different recordings of each work speak for themselves. The figures in brackets refer to the Schwann catalog entries in 1980 when most of the interviews in this book took place: *Adagio for Strings* (76) [12]; choral version as *Agnus Dei* (35) [0]; Violin Concerto (26) [1]; *Summer Music* (11) [2], *School for Scandal Overture* (11) [1]; Piano Sonata (11) [2]; *Essay for Orchestra* No. 1 (10) [0], No. 2 (9) [2], No. 3 (6) [0]; Piano Concerto (9) [2]; Cello Concerto (8) [1]; *Dover Beach* (6) [1].

---

70. On June 17, 1968, Heather Harper and Viola Tunnard performed the *Hermit Songs* in the Jubilee Hall, Aldeburgh. On June 20, 1985, in a program called "Music for a Summer Night," Jo Ann Pickens sang "Under the Willow Tree" (from *Vanessa*), "Sure on This Shining Night," and *Knoxville: Summer of 1915* with the London Mozart Players under Richard Vogt at Snape Maltings.

71. Donald Mitchell, lecture at King's College, London, October 30, 1991.

Part Two

Samuel Barber

Chapter Three

Samuel Barber Interviewed by James Fassett (1949)

CBS Radio intermission interview with James Fassett. CBS Symphony Orchestra concert conducted by Bernard Herrmann, June 19, 1949. *Knoxville: Summer of 1915*—radio premiere with Eileen Farrell.

James Fassett (1927–2009) was born in Leominster, Massachusetts, and earned degrees from Harvard and Dartmouth. He started his career as an announcer with WBZ in Boston and as a critic for *The Boston Globe*. He joined CBS Radio in 1936 and became a commentator and intermission host for the New York Philharmonic programs. From 1942 through 1963 he was director of the CBS Music Department. He was a keen ornithologist, and his *Symphony of the Birds* (1960) consisted entirely of birdcalls. He also wrote a travel book, *Italian Odyssey* (1969).

Interview

By Permission of WQXR

JF   Mr. Barber, do you recall your feelings during the very first performance of your music anywhere?

SB   No, Mr. Fassett, I don't, because I was in Italy at the time and the performance was in Philadelphia.[1]

JF   In recent years I've seen you frequently at rehearsals and performances of your music. Tell me, how much can a composer actually do when a conductor is rehearsing his music?

SB   Well, some composers have difficulties with conductors. Disagreements are bound to happen. I've found in general that conductors are very malleable. They're anxious to give a faithful performance according to

---

1. Overture to *The School for Scandal*, op. 5 (1931), which won Barber his second Joseph H. Bearns Prize in April 1933 and was premiered at Robin Hood Dell (now the Mann Center for the Performing Arts) summer series on August 30, 1933.

the composer's intentions. In fact, the better the conductor, the more anxious he seems to be to interpret exactly what the composer wishes.

JF   When was the first time you heard a piece of yours played by an orchestra?

SB   A few years after that Philadelphia performance.[2] Of course, the rehearsal is the most exciting part for the composer because then he hears for the first time the piece as he imagined it. In other words, the blueprint comes to life. But this particular rehearsal by a famous American orchestra was somewhat frustrating to me.

JF   What happened?

SB   It was the only rehearsal of the piece, and for some reason the conductor decided to work on only the first half of it. Then he sent the players home. I asked him why he hadn't even read the piece through, and he said: "Well, they'll play better tomorrow at the concert if they are just reading it!"

JF   How did the performance turn out?

SB   Oh, the piece wasn't overly difficult and it really went quite well. Anyway, it got me the Prix de Rome, so I was able to spend two years in Italy again.

JF   When you were studying in Italy, Mr. Barber, was your music performed there at all?

SB   Yes. As a matter of fact, my First Symphony was premiered in Rome by the Augusteo Orchestra under Molinari.[3]

JF   How did Italian audiences take to this new music by an American composer?

SB   Italian audiences are not used to hearing much new music, and they're not at all shy about showing their feelings. After the performance I went out onstage a couple of times and was greeted by about 50 percent applause and 50 percent hissing. I remember standing in the wings wondering whether I was supposed to go out again, and the old doorman said, "Better not—the hissers win!"

JF   What about the Italian orchestra players, did they express their like or dislike of the piece?

---

2. *Music for a Scene from Shelley*, op. 7 (1933), New York Philharmonic/Werner Janssen, Carnegie Hall, March 24, 1935.

3. *Symphony in One Movement*, op. 9, Philharmonic Augusteo Orchestra/Bernardino Molinari, Adriano Theater, Rome, December 13, 1936.

SB   Well, they were rather surprised that any American at all was writing music. I was hoping to get some encouragement from somebody, but the only thing that really happened was, right after the final rehearsal, the tuba player of the orchestra came up and congratulated me. "Maestro," he said (any musician in Italy gets called *Maestro*), "I've been waiting for a tuba part like that for fifteen years!"

JF   That should have pleased you! Many is the time I've seen composers sneaking about the corridors of Carnegie Hall trying to overhear remarks about some piece of their own they've just had performed. I've often wondered whether they find these tactics rewarding or not.

SB   It can be a little dangerous. Sometimes you hear things you'd rather not. For instance, that time in Rome, just after my symphony was performed I overheard an elderly Italian princess say, "That young man should have been strangled at birth!" I found out later that the simple townspeople who live near Salzburg were much more appreciative of music than the Roman aristocracy.

JF   You've stayed in a town near Salzburg. Did you do any composing while you were there?[4]

SB   Yes. I wrote my *Adagio for Strings* there.

JF   That was your best-known work—it's the first composition of yours I ever heard.

SB   I wish you'd hear some new ones. Everybody always plays that!

JF   Well, a good many of us heard your Second Symphony when it was broadcast during the last year of the war. You wrote it while you were in the air force, didn't you?[5]

SB   Yes, I did.

JF   How did composing and military duties mix while you were in the army?

SB   Well, my first musical assignment, which lasted some months, was moving pianos and very heavy radios that had been given to the army—you know, those awfully heavy old radios that don't work anymore.

---

4. St. Wolfgang in the Austrian Tyrol. The String Quartet, op. 11, was written between 1936 and 1938 and premiered by the Pro Arte Quartet in Rome on December 14, 1936. On November 7, 1938, Toscanini conducted the premiere of the *Adagio for Strings*, Barber's arrangement of the quartet's slow movement.

5. Second Symphony (dedicated to the Army Air Forces), op. 19, Boston Symphony Orchestra/Koussevitsky, March 3, 1944.

JF   Was that the extent of your music assignments in the army?

SB   No. The air force asked me to write a full-length symphony.

JF   Did they leave you alone when you wrote it?

SB   Not exactly. I had to report every two weeks and play what I had written to a colonel. As it was one of my most complicated works, I had no idea what he expected to hear. I rather thought it might be something like "You're in the Army Now."[6] So I was a little nervous when I reported to play for him on a battered-up piano in the back of an army theater. All he said was: "Well, corporal, it's not quite what we expected from you. Since the air force uses all sorts of the most modern technical devices, I hope you'll write this symphony in quarter-tones. But do what you can, do what you can, corporal."

JF   What was the reaction of army brass after the performance of the symphony?

SB   Well, a general's wife introduced herself to me on the steps of Symphony Hall in Boston just before the performance and said, "Tell me, corporal, did you learn to write symphonies in the air force, or did you know something about music before you went in the service?" I answered, "I'm afraid I was a musician before I went into the army." She said, "I thought so, corporal." One of the strangest letters I received after this performance was from a Chinese corporal in the American Army who wrote to me saying that although he disliked my symphony intensely, he applauded vociferously because he thought that all corporals should be encouraged!

JF   Tell us a little bit about *Knoxville: Summer of 1915,* with the text by James Agee. How did you happen to select it for a musical setting?[7]

SB   I had always admired Mr. Agee's writing, and this prose poem particularly struck me because the summer evening he describes in his native southern town reminded me so much of similar evenings when I was a child at home. I found out after setting this that Mr. Agee and I are the same age, and the year he describes, 1915, was when we were both five.

---

6. Popular song recorded on November 27, 1940, by Abe Lyman and his Californians, vocals by The Chorus, on Bluebird B-10971-B.

7. James Agee (1909–55), American novelist and poet who also worked in films. His prose poem "Knoxville: Summer of 1915" was written in 1935. Barber's setting, op. 24 (1948), was premiered by Eleanor Steber with the Boston Symphony/Koussevitsky on April 9, 1948.

JF   I see there's a motto on the score:

We are talking now of summer evenings in Knoxville, Tennessee,
and the time that I lived there so successfully disguised to myself
as a child.

SB   Yes. It seemed to set the mood for the piece. You see, it expresses a
child's feeling of loneliness, wonder, and lack of identity in that marginal
world between twilight and sleep.

[The interview concluded with Fassett and Barber reading portions of the text.]

Chapter Four

Samuel Barber Interviewed by Robert Sherman (1978)

WQXR Great Artists Series, September 30, 1978, before the premiere of Barber's *Third Essay for Orchestra,* op. 47, by the New York Philharmonic under Zubin Mehta.

Robert Sherman (1932–) was born in New York City and is a widely known radio presenter. He has hosted the McGraw-Hill Companies' Young Artists Showcase on WQXR for over thirty years, and *Woody's Children,* which reflects his interest in folk music, reached its forty-first anniversary in 2010. He has taught the Business of Music course at Juilliard since 1992. His mother was the pianist Nadia Reisenberg and his aunt, Clara Rockmore, was the pioneering virtuoso on the theremin.

Interview

By Permission of WQXR

RS   It's been a long time between your *Second Essay* and your *Third.*[1]

SB   There were a couple of operas that sort of slipped in there!

RS   We've talked with a number of composers here, and one of the issues that comes up again and again is the question of performance. It's on the premiere that a work is judged. Have you been short-changed with some performances?

SB   I think I have been very, very lucky in general and especially for symphonic or concert pieces. I've had perfectly marvelous conductors, pianists, and singers. I think that my operas have had ups and downs.

RS   Have you any theories about why contemporary opera is not more successful?

SB   I have no theories about contemporary opera at all, but I know that an opera consists of many, many things from stagehands on to the designer of the sets to the possibilities of the prima donna being able to act—or not. Even so, I've had perfectly marvelous performances. The first

---

1. *Essay for Orchestra,* op. 12 (1937); *Second Essay for Orchestra,* op. 19 (1944).

performance of *Vanessa* at the Metropolitan was everything I wished I could have had—except that, of course, there were three changes of cast. There were three different Vanessas before the gallant Eleanor Steber stepped in.[2] With the stage sets of *Antony and Cleopatra* I was not very happy. There were a great number of things going on on the stage. You could hardly hear the music. I think Leontyne Price told me she held on to her wig, decided it was either the opera or herself, or the music. I forget which it was. She was very gallant about that. I thought that was mistreated by the man who did the sets, who shall be nameless.[3]

RS   In the 1974 revival at the Juilliard, you seemed much more content.

SB   That's right. There I was very happy because they took away all the fussiness, the elephants—I forget what they were—at the premiere. That, I think, proved something about the work itself.

RS   Are there some of your works that haven't been given enough attention?

SB   The *Adagio for Strings* seems to go along quite well. I would like to have a record of all my songs—there is none.[4] That's odd because they're sung a lot. Let me see what else I can think of to complain about. Very little!

RS   Did you get the idea of expanding the *Adagio for Strings* for string orchestra early on?

SB   Rodzinsky at Salzburg suggested I write a piece for Toscanini, who was then doing the NBC Orchestra, and I wrote *Essay No. 1.* The new piece we're talking about is *Essay No. 3,* so I've been at that title for some time. Many years—I can't count. The *Adagio* was the slow movement of a quartet and I just arranged it for strings, and in that way it's been much more known. Toscanini played both pieces actually in the same program. I was very surprised.

RS   That must have been a great adventure, since he wasn't given to performing much American music.

SB   It was. I had sent the scores to him and I had no answer. The chauffeur brought them back, which was not a good sign, and Mr. Toscanini left for Italy. I was going over with Menotti to see him at the Isolino di San Giovanni where he lived. I knew him a little bit. Then I decided I wouldn't go because I was annoyed that he'd never even given me an

---

2. Eleanor Steber (1914–90), American operatic soprano who gave the premiere of *Knoxville: Summer of 1915* in 1948 and took the title role in *Vanessa* at only six weeks' notice in 1957.

3. Franco Zeffirelli (1923–), prominent Italian film and opera director.

4. Cheryl Studer, soprano, Thomas Hampson, baritone, John Browning, piano, and the Emerson String Quartet recorded the complete published songs in 1994. Deutsche Grammophon 435 867–62.

answer. At the end Toscanini said to Menotti, "Where is your friend Barber?" Gian Carlo said, "He's not feeling very well today." Toscanini said, "I don't believe that. He's mad at me. Tell him not to be mad. I'm not going to play one of his pieces, I'm going to play both." That was very good news. I sat in a hotel in Pallanza waiting for the boat to get back, and it came back with extremely good news.

[recording of Toscanini's performance of the *Adagio for Strings*]

RS So you were no longer annoyed with Toscanini?

SB No, no. Not a bit. [*laughs*]

RS We're going to hear some songs recorded some years ago and never released. This must have been very frustrating.

SB It was. Poulenc was the pianist, the baritone Bernac—and I was the page turner![5] [*laughs*] I couldn't understand why it took twenty years to get this record out, but it's just come out now.[6] I'm very pleased with that. It's in French, which is perhaps odd.

RS Does the text matter, or is it a musical evocation of a mood?

SB Oh, no, no; the text means a great deal to me. I read lots of poetry anyway, so I go through tons and tons of poems that could possibly be songs. It's very hard to find them—they are either too wordy, too introverted, or what have you.

RS How many songs have you written altogether?

SB I really don't know. Maybe fifty. I'm not sure. But there again I shouldn't complain. I've had wonderful performances. Leontyne has done two cycles, Fischer-Dieskau did a cycle, but I would like to have them all on one record.[7] That's just really being troublesome! [*laughs*]

The text of *Mélodies passagères* is by Rainer Maria Rilke.[8] He wrote it in French because he was at that time the secretary of Rodin in Paris. I was a little bit hesitant about writing in French—although I know French—but setting French to music is ticklish. The French are very, very particular about it. On the other hand, I felt "why not," so I plunged in and did these *Mélodies passagères*.

[recording of *Mélodies passagères* with Bernac and Poulenc]

---

5. Francis Poulenc (1900–1963) and Pierre Bernac (1899–1979) had a distinguished recital partnership.

6. Recorded on February 15, 1952; released on New World Records NW-229 in 1978.

7. For Leontyne Price: *Hermit Songs*, op. 29 (1953), and *Despite and Still*, op. 41 (1968). For Dietrich Fischer-Dieskau: *Three Songs*, op. 45 (1972).

8. Rainer Maria Rilke (1875–1926), German lyric poet. *Mélodies passagères*, op. 27 (1951).

SB   Do you know the real reason that I wrote that in French? [*hesitation*] It was because I was in love in Paris. How can you not be in love in Paris?

RS   It's twenty-six years since that recording was made. How do the songs seem to you now?

SB   I think it's beautiful; they sang them so well.

Poulenc was a good friend, one of my only composer friends, I would say. He dedicated a piece to me and I dedicated these songs to him.[9] He was a wonderful combination of a *boulevardier*—a very worldly Frenchman— and also religious. He sent me down to a place called Rocamadour, which I thought was just dreadful. It was in a ravine someplace where he had had a large statue in silver put in the chapel.[10] He was very, very serious about his religion. No fooling there. You hear that in the music.

RS   Many young composers today seem to change styles regularly. Is this a trend of our times or nothing new?

SB   I think it's a sense of desperation that is not too fortunate. I can only say that I myself wrote always as I wished—as I wanted to for myself—without a tremendous desire to find the latest thing possible.

RS   To what extent do you take the words of critics to heart?

SB   Very little. I once learned from Albert Spalding that the best thing to do with reviews was to pay no attention but to measure how long they are.[11] I've told that to many young composers, but nobody ever listens!

RS   After the current premiere, won't you dive for the papers the next day?

SB   No.

RS   You really won't?

SB   Sometimes I did and sometimes I didn't. For operas you get terribly curious about what's going to happen, but very often I just don't read them at all—then sometimes I cheat and read them.

RS   Does the American composer of today have the stature he had twenty or thirty years ago?

---

9. Poulenc dedicated his *Capriccio d'après "Le bal masqué"* for two pianos (1953) to Barber.

10. Poulenc wrote his *Litanies à la vierge noire* (Notre Dame de Rocamadour) for voices and organ in 1936. Rocamadour, in southwest France, contains the Church of Notre Dame with its wooden black Madonna that has attracted pilgrims for centuries.

11. Albert Spalding (1888–1953), American violinist who gave the premiere of Barber's Violin Concerto.

SB   I would say yes in some cases. Even more. I think it was not so easy twenty or thirty years ago.

RS   Have recordings made a difference?

SB   That's helped a great deal.

RS   Why did you become a composer? You were a pianist and a singer?

SB   I was not a singer; I was seven years old when I began composing and improvising at the piano—the usual story. I was supposed to be a doctor, to go to Princeton; everything I was supposed to do I didn't! I was very lucky because the Curtis Institute opened its doors in 1924 when I was fourteen, and Mrs. Bok started that extraordinary school just thirty miles from my house. So I went there and had wonderful teachers. I was very lucky. I think I was very lucky always.

RS   You've mentioned that before.

SB   Well, a lot of people complain so much. I don't think I'm a complainer.

RS   Have you pushed your own music? You seem modest and un-pushy.

SB   I don't think I'm very modest, but I was lucky to have the same publisher all my life: Schirmer. I went to them and I think I took twelve songs in, and they turned down nine and took three.[12] From there on I've been with them.

RS   Did you give the other nine back later?

SB   No, never. They were right to turn them down!

RS   Do you have unpublished pieces in a trunk someplace?

SB   I have an awfully nice new trunk but nothing in it! [*laughs*]

      Horowitz had a great influence on me for writing for piano—good God! He taught me so much. He used to play Scriabin for me all night in Mt. Kisco.[13] My piano teacher Vengerova was a great teacher: she taught Lenny Bernstein and Lukas Foss.[14]

RS   Was the sonata written with Horowitz in mind?

SB   No, I think I just started to write a sonata. Then I got to the third movement. There's a funny story about that. I played it for him at his house

---

12.   *Three Songs*, op. 2.

13.   Alexander Scriabin (1872–1915), advanced Russian composer with a large piano output.

14.   Isabelle Vengerova (1877–1956), Russian pianist and teacher, pupil of Theodor Leschetizky, who came to the United States in 1923 and taught Barber from 1926 to 1931.

and I fell on the floor at the end of the third movement—that was really just a joke, but they were a little worried about me. It was awfully hard! Then came a period when I couldn't think of what to do for the fourth movement. Mrs. Horowitz called me up and said: "The trouble with you is that you are a *stitico*"—it means constipated—"That's what you are—a constipated composer!" [*laughs*] That was the fugue that then appeared. That made me so mad that I ran up to my studio and wrote it the next day! That has kept plenty of pianists busy since.

[recording of Piano Sonata finale with Horowitz]

RS   Do you compose to a schedule or work to deadlines?

SB   I would say a bit of both. If I have a deadline, then of course I have to meet it. Most of the time I have. I think the Philharmonic is now asking me whether I ever didn't meet a deadline. I won't tell them!

RS   What are the works you are contemplating now?

SB   Oboe Concerto—a concertino for oboe, which the Philharmonic will do in February. It's the farewell performance of Harold Gomberg who's an old friend of mine.[15] We were together in Curtis days. So I have two pieces at the Philharmonic this year, and that's all I have in my schedule.

RS   But what about things in compositional stages of one sort or another?

SB   What do you mean?

RS   What are you planning? What can we look for next year?

SB   I don't plan anything. I don't think I plan anything.

RS   You mean you don't have thoughts kicking around that are going to germinate some day?

SB   No, no. I really don't.

RS   So you wait until . . .

---

15. Harold Gomberg (1916–85) was principal oboe with the New York Philharmonic during the years 1943–77. Barbara Heyman has commented: "Barber lived to complete only the slow movement of the concerto and suggested that Charles Turner should orchestrate it as a single movement. Barber did create a short score and lived long enough to correct Schirmer proofs. Unfortunately, Turner did not include the cadenza that Barber wrote for Gomberg, the location of which is clearly marked in the score." E-mail to me, July 13, 2009. Andrew Porter heard the premiere given by the New York Philharmonic on December 17–19, 1981. See "Graceful, Passionate, Poetic," in *Musical Events: A Chronicle 1980–1983* (New York: Simon and Schuster, 1987), 190–91.

SB   Till something happens in my mind, and then I do it. If nothing happens in my mind, I don't do it!

RS   What do you do with the rest of your time if something is not happening?

SB   I don't teach, for which I feel somewhat guilty. I really don't want to teach. I don't have any pedagogical feelings, really. I read a great deal, I walk a lot, I have a house in Italy in the mountains,[16] and I watch Italian politics with some trepidation.

RS   You could have a subject for another opera there!

SB   Yes, you certainly could!

---

16. At Santa Cristina in the Dolomites, northern Italy.

Chapter Five

Samuel Barber Interviewed by Allan Kozinn (1979)

Barber's interview with Allan Kozinn (1954–) took place at the end of December 1979. Because of reports of his illness, there was some question of whether he would go through with the interview, since a few weeks earlier he had canceled most of his appointments. However, pianist-composer Philip Ramey convinced Barber not to break this appointment, and the result was the last interview he ever gave. Originally, his meeting with Kozinn was to have taken place at Barber's Fifth Avenue apartment in New York, but, because of construction there to try and shield his working area from distracting traffic noise, they met at the offices of G. Schirmer. It was a cold, gray, windy day, but Barber appeared to be in good health and good spirits, although his final illness would soon take its toll.

Allan Kozinn is one of the leading music critics on the New York scene. He graduated from Syracuse University with degrees in music and journalism in 1976 and started to write for *The New York Times* the following year. He has also been a contributing editor for *High Fidelity, Opus,* and *Keynote* and was the first music critic for the *New York Observer.* His articles and reviews have also appeared in *Opera News, Stereo Review, The Listener* (BBC), *The Los Angeles Times, Musical America, Guitar Review, Fugue and Keyboard,* and in other publications in the United States, Europe, and Japan. He joined the faculty at New York University in 2004 and has also taught at the Juilliard School. His books include *The New York Times Essential Library: Classical Music* (2004), *The Beatles* (1995), *Mischa Elman and the Romantic Style* (1990), and *The Guitar: The History, the Players, the Music* (1984).

Interview

By Permission of Allan Kozinn

AK   In 1935 you told an interviewer that there were fine opportunities for young composers and that American music could be expected to make great progress. How does it look forty-five years later?

SB   I'm not very good at summing these things up or comparing one period to another because I don't think historically. But I do think it's much harder for a young composer now than it was when I was starting out. First of all, there were conductors back then who were interested in American music—Koussevitzky, for example. When young conductors tell me they have trouble designing programs, I always tell them to look at the Boston/Koussevitzky programs. They were superb: they had the classics, the romantics, and almost every program had an American work. But that's all gone.

AK   Why has that kind of programming disappeared?

SB   I don't know. Why don't you ask Mr. Muti? He came over to take a nice American post, as successor to Ormandy, and announced in a *New York Times* interview that he's never conducted an American work in his life! Well, that's the end of us in Philadelphia—my hometown.

AK   Once he's on the Philadelphia podium he'll have to conduct some American music eventually?

SB   I rather doubt it.[1] It seems many of today's conductors are too lazy to learn new things. And it's not just laziness. They are not at all convinced that new music is any good. Therefore, new works only get done when the wives of composers pressure the members of an orchestra's board of directors to have certain works played. That's why I advise all young composers to get married as early as possible!

AK   You've never married.

SB   No.

AK   And you don't have that much trouble getting your music performed.

SB   Well, sometimes I do. Just recently, a piece of mine called *Die Natali* was canceled by the Philadelphia Orchestra. They said that they only had five rehearsals and that would not be sufficient time to prepare the piece. It's difficult—Charles Munch, who conducted the premiere with the Boston Symphony, told me it was difficult.[2] And there are plenty of other works of mine that I wish would be performed more often. Or better yet, I wish they'd be recorded so that I wouldn't have to bother with them any more. Once they're on record, young musicians can

---

1. Riccardo Muti (1941–), Italian conductor who was music director of the Philadelphia Orchestra from 1980 to 1992. In fact, he did subsequently commission a succession of new works.

2. *Die Natali*, chorale preludes for Christmas, op. 37 (1960). A Koussevitzky commission premiered by the Boston Symphony Orchestra on December 22 and 23, 1960.

hear the works and decide whether they want to learn them, even if the orchestras don't routinely play them. But the recording situation is miserable and getting worse.

AK   Can you suggest a solution?

SB   I wish—and I think all composers wish—that a certain amount of money could be put aside by foundations simply for the recording of a good first performance. And then the recordings should be distributed well. Not just to schools and libraries; that's not enough. It doesn't give the works any exposure. They should be distributed by the major companies.

AK   I think the New World Records project is a step in that direction

SB   Yes, but New World Records is a mysterious label, and you can't get copies of its recordings unless you're connected with a library or educational institution. They put out a disc that contained my old recording of *Dover Beach,* and although it was my own performance of my own work, they didn't even want to let me have a copy at first! I told them I'd be perfectly willing to buy it, and eventually I got one. The idea of the project is fine. But what's the use if people can't get copies?[3]

AK   How did that recording of *Dover Beach* come about?

SB   Someone at Victor liked my voice and thought they were signing up a new John McCormack.[4] Well, they didn't get one! *Dover Beach* is a very difficult piece because nobody is boss, so to speak—not the singer or the string quartet. It's chamber music. And since we recorded it in the days of 78s, when somebody made a mistake we had to go back to the beginning. Not being a trained singer, I ran out of voice after the third time, but there was always something wrong. When we finally got a good performance, the second violinist, at the very end, hit his music stand with his bow. So, you hear this little "ting" like a triangle. But I wasn't about to do the piece again, so that "clink" sound is still on the record. Maybe it helps.

AK   I believe you've tried to create opportunities for unknown composers. Wasn't the commission of *Summer Music* [1955] tied to some such scheme?

----

3. New World Records, Recorded Anthology of American Music, Inc., was founded in 1975 by the Rockefeller Foundation with a mandate to produce a hundred records of American music distributed free of charge to almost seven thousand colleges worldwide. That task was completed in 1978, and the company went on to produce over 250 further titles, including Barber's *Antony and Cleopatra.* Since Barber made his comments, the availability of this catalog on CD has been widespread and influential; the whole scene has changed.

4. John McCormack (1884–1945), celebrated Irish tenor.

SB   Yes. That was commissioned by the Chamber Music Society of Detroit, and the idea was that instead of paying me my usual fee, the members of the Society and the people who came to the concert would each contribute something like five dollars toward the work. I was hoping that this practice would catch on, that music societies in small towns all over the country would take up similar collections and use the funds to commission works from young local composers who needed experience and exposure and would therefore write for a comparatively small fee just to hear their music performed. I made a speech against myself, essentially, and told them it was crazy that they didn't use local composers. It was certainly done in Bach's day. But they didn't like that. They just wanted the same tired old names—Copland, Sessions, Harris, me, et cetera—so the idea never got off the ground. Consequently, not only are the young composers not getting the commissions, but the prices for new works are staying rather high. In fact, I've done my best to increase them—which I guess ruins my story!

AK   Was *Summer Music* intended as an aural description of summer sounds?

SB   It's supposed to be evocative of summer—summer meaning languid, not [*claps loudly*] killing mosquitoes! I think Henry Cowell once wrote a piece in which the orchestra members had to clap their hands as if to kill mosquitoes—"brilliant invention," the critics called it.[5] But, really, there's not much to say about *Summer Music* except that everybody plays it too slowly, which leads certain charming colleagues of mine to come up with real[ly] mean remarks. A couple of them came up to me after a performance at Tanglewood and told me that it dragged so it should have been called *Winter Music!* But that was because they didn't play up to my tempos. Just about the only performance I can recall hearing at the right speed was by the New York Woodwind Quintet at the University of Missouri.

AK   Why is it usually done so slowly?

SB   Well, it's hard for the wind players to keep up with it, or so I'm told. But people always use that as an excuse. Not long ago, the bassoon player of the Philadelphia Orchestra told me that *Summer Music* is in the repertoire of every wind quintet, so it can't be that difficult. I think the problem is, again, laziness.

AK   Does it seem to you that the level of performance, particularly of younger players, has improved dramatically in the last decade or so?

---

5. Henry Cowell (1897–1965) developed avant-garde techniques in the 1920s but later drew on non-Western musics to create a music of the whole world.

SB   Yes. That's an encouraging thing. Young players have made extraordi-
      nary progress, musically and technically. I remember when my Piano
      Sonata [1949] had its first performance, by Horowitz. An eminent
      critic, now deceased—I love quoting deceased critics, the more the
      merrier!—said that the sonata would rarely be played and certainly
      not as it was by Horowitz, who made it into the fine work it is, but one
      doubts if anyone else can play it. Well, the joke, of course, is that now
      the sonata is a required work on just about every piano competition,
      and young people have no trouble at all with it. I get letters from peo-
      ple saying "please, please, write something else for the piano, we're get-
      ting sick of that fugue." On the other hand, I don't like it when they're
      too confident either.

AK   How do you mean, too confident?

SB   Sometimes I get tired of hearing the *Adagio for Strings* all the time. But I
      amuse myself during the performances because I know there's going to
      be a mistake somewhere, and I just wait for it to happen. It's such an easy
      work that they never bother to rehearse it.

AK   Are there specific trouble spots?

SB   No, but there are lots of whole notes in the score, and orchestra psychol-
      ogy is rather funny. When they see whole notes they think, "Oh, we don't
      have to look at the conductor here." And invariably, a viola or a second
      violin will make a mistake. It happens at every performance.

AK   Early in your career, you performed yourself. Why did you stop?

SB   Because onstage I have about as much projection as a baby skunk! Also, I
      got bored with rehearsing my own music. Some composers adore it, but I
      don't find it very interesting. There's a lack, in me, of pedagogical talent.
      And when you're guest conducting, you don't have the kind of author-
      ity over an orchestra that its regular conductor has—and you need that
      authority to make them do it right. Toscanini would just get up there and
      scream "Stupidi! Imbecilli!" and throw down his watch! I've seen him do
      that. But he was Toscanini and it was his orchestra. They wouldn't dare
      make the mistakes with him that they'd make with me.

AK   Do you think that as the composer your interpretations were definitive?

SB   My tempos could be definitive. But generally I don't believe composers
      make very good conductors. Someone who conducts every day can give
      a technically superior performance. I remember, the last work of mine I
      conducted was my Second Symphony, with the Boston Symphony. I had
      conducted it in Denmark and in England, and by the time I got to Bos-
      ton I knew exactly where the violas would go wrong and where I'd have

to have them do it over and over, very slowly. Now, how can you remain interested in doing that, whether it's your own music or not?

AK   You withdrew the Second Symphony?

SB   That's right. I realized one that day that it really wasn't very good, so I got hold of all the copies here at Schirmer's, and I burned them. We used to have fun here in those days![6]

AK   Which pieces, by contrast, are you fond of?

SB   Well, I'm not exactly an arsonist. There are some works I'm close to—*Knoxville*, the Piano Sonata, the Piano Concerto, and *Vanessa*. By the way, *Vanessa* was composed without a commission. I just wanted to see if I could write an opera. I remember bringing the score to Rudolf Bing, at the Met, and having to play it for him on the piano, singing all the parts, while he turned pages. That was not an easy job!

AK   When most composers won't write a string quartet without a commission, you wrote an opera—the most difficult form—without knowing if and when it would be performed?

SB   That's true. Opera is the most slippery thing that you can get into. There are more excuses for not doing it or doing it badly. But I've always been a sucker for opera. It's terribly exhilarating when you finally hear and see it onstage, with all the costumes and lights.

AK   Why have you done only two?

SB   I've had a difficult time finding librettos that interest me.

AK   How did you and Menotti come to collaborate on *Vanessa*?

SB   We were living in the same house at the time—Capricorn at Mt. Kisco—and summers we were renting a cottage in Maine. There was always a problem with hearing each other working. One summer there were four of us, each trying to keep the others quiet! Menotti was working on something, I was starting *Vanessa*, Thomas Schippers was learning *Salome*, and there was someone else. It was very noisy, ruined my summer. Capricorn solved all that because it has two wings and we could work without disturbing each other.

AK   Did Menotti have any input into *Vanessa*'s music, or was that against the ground rules?

SB   No, not a bit. There were no ground rules, but Menotti was busy with projects of his own. So he would write the words in a little notebook and

---

6. This is hyperbole! See interview with Hans W. Heinsheimer in chapter 15.

send them over to me. Of course, I would always show him the music. He's a wonderful critic and quite a good teacher. He has a superb sense of line.

AK   Sense of line along with traditional harmonic and melodic style have marked your work. Have you ever been tempted to explore some of the more avant-garde sonorities and styles?

SB   Ah, I was waiting for this! Do you mean "why haven't I changed?" Why should I? There's no reason music should be difficult for the audience, is there?

AK   No. Do you address the audience when you compose?

SB   No, I address myself. Myself and Helen Carter! She's the judge. After all, she once announced that all American composers are dead, except, of course, her husband, Elliott.[7] So we have to take our music to her, and she tells us what to do with it.

AK   I see. Do you follow the music of people in the Elliott Carter school?

SB   No, though I must admit I have not heard any new composers whose music has interested me very much. I know some names, and I've listened to some records. But after one hearing I've had it. They don't seem to be developing very much. So, sorry, but I can't say anything about composers I think may be the big ones of the new generation. Let's leave that to the musicologists. They know everything![8]

---

7. Elliott Carter (1908–) celebrated his hundredth birthday in 2008.

8. Barber was equally dismissive after his publisher Edward Murphy sent him tickets for *Sweeney Todd*, which premiered on March 1, 1979. On March 26 Barber wrote: "It is undeniable that Sondheim has talent and wit, but I missed the Music. I wish that someplace, somewhere there were a tune that one could sing or hum going out of the theater. This was totally lacking. Production splendid, orchestration good. The work is tricky and difficult; and, without Angela Lansbury, I really doubt if it will be used very much. I dislike taking a negative point [of] view since I feel Sondheim really is talented and certainly should be carefully watched, if not grabbed, if such were your intention." Murphy, e-mail to me, May 27, 2009.

Part Three

Friends

Chapter Six

Gian Carlo Menotti

Interview with Peter Dickinson, Yester House, Gifford, Scotland, April 6, 1981

Introduction

Gian Carlo Menotti (1911–2007) was one of the most successful opera composers of the mid-twentieth century. He had an inborn sense of the theater, inheriting the tradition of Puccini, with an intuitive feel for character and drama as a fusion of music and theater to his own texts—almost all in English. Menotti remained Italian to the core, even though he spent most of his life based in America before, improbably, buying a country mansion in Scotland. The relationship between Menotti and Barber was crucial to the development of both composers—their work is at the core of mid-twentieth-century music as perceived by a wide public—so Menotti's background is particularly relevant to any study of Barber.

Menotti was born in Cadegliano, on Lake Lugano, on July 7, 1911, and died in Monte Carlo on February 1, 2007. He was the sixth of eight surviving children in a large family network. His mother, Ines, was the predominant parental influence; she gave her children the chance to learn various instruments and pampered Gian Carlo. Samuel Barber, Menotti's almost lifelong partner, felt she was "made to be the heroine of a Puccini opera."[1]

When his family moved to Milan, Gian Carlo was a regular attendee at theaters as well as opera at La Scala. As he explained, it was a surprise when his mother decided to send him to the Curtis Institute in Philadelphia. Another shock was the death of Menotti's father and his mother's remarriage to a much younger man. The couple went to live in South America and, in 1928, left Menotti in Philadelphia at age seventeen.

By a charmed coincidence, he encountered Barber. At Curtis they shared a composition teacher, Rosario Scalero, benefiting from his solid traditional approach. Then the two young composers went out to explore the world

---

1. Cited in John Gruen, *Menotti: A Biography* (New York: Macmillan, 1978), 23.

together. In 1934 they spent the winter in Vienna. Two years later they took a cottage in St. Wolfgang for the summer, where Menotti wrote *Amelia al ballo* (*Amelia Goes to the Ball*) based on familiar scenes from Austrian life, and Barber wrote his String Quartet, out of which would come his celebrated *Adagio for Strings*. The premiere of *Amelia* was at the Philadelphia Academy, and the New York production a few days later was so successful that the Met offered to produce it—in a double bill with Strauss's *Elektra*—in 1938. This made Menotti's name. *The New York Times* recognized "something that has not materialized so far from an American-born composer" and admired Menotti's flexibility and spontaneity.[2] The Italian premiere seemed set, but Menotti refused to join the Fascist party, which caused him to be passed over in his own country until the end of the war.

The success of *Amelia* led to an NBC Radio commission, *The Old Maid and the Thief*, which has been regularly performed—especially by students and amateurs—ever since. Encouraged by Menotti's growing public, the Met came back for a full-length opera. This time, with *The Island God*, the composer went in for *opera seria* and miscalculated. He believed he was ostracized socially for what was regarded as a failure, something Barber would experience after *Antony and Cleopatra*.

Menotti's next operatic opportunity was *The Medium*, a two-act tragedy to his own libretto, premiered at Columbia University in 1946. Virgil Thomson, in *The New York Herald Tribune*, commended the "frankly Italianate treatment of ordinary human beings as thoroughly interesting in every way,"[3] but *The Medium* was not fully launched until it formed a double bill with *The Telephone* at the Ethel Barrymore Theater on Broadway. Even then, ticket sales were weak and the backers were losing money until Toscanini, who had crucially supported Barber, once again took a hand in Menotti's fortunes. With characteristic subtlety, Menotti told him of the performance but said that naturally he did not expect the great conductor to come. The ruse worked: Toscanini came, adored the opera, and came twice more. The press took up the whole story and the double bill became a sellout, running for eight months. Chandler Cowles, one of Menotti's backers, found him to be "a combination of a saint and a devil. He is capable of the most extraordinary kindness and sensitivity. At other times he can be full of intrigue."[4]

The Medium was filmed and toured in Europe by the U.S. State Department. *The Consul*, four years later, also made a major impact, receiving a Pulitzer Prize and the Drama Critics Circle Award. The composer was responsible for everything—the play, the music, the casting, and stage direction. The text has been translated into twelve languages and the opera produced in more than

2. Cited in ibid., 35.
3. Cited in ibid., 63.
4. Cited in ibid., 67.

twenty countries. Next came *Amahl and the Night Visitors,* the Christmas story commissioned by NBC as the first-ever TV opera. It brought Menotti an even wider public, with continual international success because of the story's touching immediacy. *The Saint of Bleecker Street* played on Broadway less spectacularly than *The Medium* did but still lasted four months and collected two awards and another Pulitzer Prize in 1955.

In 1958 Menotti inaugurated the Festival of Two Worlds at the Umbrian hilltown Spoleto; in 1977 he expanded it to Charleston, South Carolina. When Barber was asked why Menotti wanted to involve himself in such a time-consuming operation, he said: "You could say it's a need for having people around all of the time. A need for a certain amount of power."[5] Menotti himself explained that he started the festival "for the joy of it," but looking back in 2001 he admitted, "I think I've wasted too much time looking for money or making programs and trying to bewitch artists to come here for nothing."

All of this activity coincided with changes of fashion, which told against both Menotti and Barber. Menotti's interest in being useful and relevant led him toward a series of children's operas such as *Martin's Lie.* Impressed by Menotti's flair, Stravinsky specifically asked for him to direct *The Rake's Progress* at the Hamburg Opera in 1967. This led to Menotti's own *Help! Help! The Globolinks,* another children's opera, written for the same theater and produced the following year. In 1984 Menotti received the Kennedy Center Honor for lifetime achievement in the arts, and he continued to write operas through the 1980s.

From 1943 until 1973, Menotti and Barber lived at their house called Capricorn (also the name of Barber's *Capricorn Concerto,* op. 41) in Mt. Kisco, New York.[6] The sale of the house and the breakup of their partnership were major shocks for Barber especially and may have contributed to his decline. Menotti, who gave a frank interview to *The New York Times* near his sixtieth birthday in 1971,[7] resented some of the carping reviews he began getting from New York critics in the late 1960s and decided to leave America.

A strange twist of fantasy took Menotti to Scotland, where he bought Yester House, the Palladian ancestral home of the Marquess of Tweeddale. Menotti tried to explain his move: "I've chosen to live here, so I could be completely cut off from my past. It was a desire to find a place where I could hide."[8] Another unexpected turn of events was his meeting with Francis Phelan, who became the composer's adopted son in 1974.[9]

---

5. Cited in ibid., 46.

6. Designed by William Lescaze (1896–1969), Swiss architect who moved to the United States in 1920.

7. "And Where Do You Run at 60?" *The New York Times,* July 18, 1971, reprinted in Gruen, *Menotti: A Biography,* 193–96.

8. Cited in ibid., xiii.

9. Ibid., 181–85.

Menotti had a generous and often amusing disposition. When he came to take part in my program at the Institute of United States Studies at the University of London on November 3, 1998, to hear the British premiere of his Trio for violin, clarinet, and piano by the Verdehr Trio he said, "Unlike Victorian children, old composers should be heard and not seen." He added modestly that he knew he wasn't Bach but felt he wasn't Offenbach either.

The reaction against Menotti's popularity has been disproportionate. The movement toward neoromanticism in the late twentieth century tended to favor Barber. But for sheer theatrical craft and human curiosity, Menotti created a telling *verismo* of the World War II era. He frequently promoted the careers of others, had a rare zest for living, and kept opera alive, reaching a wide public at a difficult time in the mid-twentieth century.

Interview

By Permission of Francis Menotti

PD What was it like arriving at the Curtis Institute in Philadelphia in 1928 when you first met Barber?[10]

GCM First of all, it should not surprise you that I went to study in America because not only then but even now musical education in Italy was very poor. Toscanini advised my mother to send me to America because he knew how mediocre Italian conservatoires were—and still are. So I was dumped by my mother in Philadelphia at the Curtis Institute, and I had an Italian teacher—Rosario Scalero—who taught both me and Sam. He was a pupil of Mandyczewski in Vienna, so we were brought up in the Viennese School of composition.[11]

I arrived and I spoke very little English. The very first person I met in the school was Samuel Barber because he was the only pupil there who spoke fluent French and Italian. We became friends almost immediately and remained friends for the rest of his life.[12]

---

10. Orlando Cole, cellist, was also a fellow student of Barber's. See his 2005 interview in chapter 17.

11. Eusebius Mandyczewski (1857–1929), Austrian musicologist, friend of Brahms. In 1928 Barber visited Mandyczewski who lived outside Vienna; Heyman, *Samuel Barber: The Composer and His Music*, 57. Menotti told Fegley on December 9, 1981, that Scalero was very severe as a teacher of harmony and counterpoint and focused on the quality of basic ideas. Once, when Menotti was desperate, Barber wrote his motet assignment for him.

12. Barber also spoke German and Menotti told Fegley that he could make himself understood in Russian, too, which came in useful when Barber met Nikita Khrushchev in

PD   What sort of American was he at that time?

GCM He was extremely well-read; he had traveled; he was very spoiled because
     he was meant to be very good-looking and had so many talents. He had
     a beautiful baritone voice—heard in the recording of *Dover Beach*—and
     was a pupil of the Spanish baritone Emilio di Gogorza, one of the great
     lieder singers at the time.[13] He was also an extraordinarily good pianist,
     a pupil of Madame Vengerova, and, of course, a star composer.[14] He was
     one of the favorite pupils of the conservatory.[15]

     I remember that when we met and became friends he made fun of me
     because I came from Milan and my musical education consisted mainly
     of opera and the usual Mozart, Beethoven, and so on. At that time I
     hardly knew Brahms at all because in Italy Brahms was considered a
     very academic and boring composer. My friendship with Sam developed
     under the wings of Brahms's music—he introduced me to Brahms whom
     he adored at that time.[16]

PD   So, is his early music Brahmsian? The *School for Scandal Overture,* for
     example? *Dover Beach?*

GCM There's certainly a Brahmsian influence, especially in the Cello Concerto
     and in many of the pieces that remain unpublished. As I'm the executor of
     his will, I'm in the very difficult position of having to decide whether to pub-
     lish some of that early music, some of which is really lovely—but very Brahm-
     sian! You can hear the influence of Brahms in almost every measure.

PD   What's surprising is that the early music is so polished. It's all there, with
     no casting around. How did that happen?

1961 when he was the first American composer invited to the Congress of Soviet Composers. Soon after arriving in Philadelphia, Menotti was regularly invited to visit Barber's family. Sam was a great giggler, so it was fatal for them to sit together in church; they had to be
separated by Barber's parents. Even when Barber was away at the American Academy in
Rome for one winter in 1936, Menotti went to see his family. When they were both in Italy,
Barber became part of Menotti's large family, where he was known as Uncle Sam. Menotti
said that Barber was impractical, hated mechanical things like automats, and when travel-
ing was in danger of losing his passport. He suffered from hay fever.

    13. Emilio di Gogorza taught Barber from 1926 to 1930. He was an operatic baritone
who made early recordings with Caruso and taught in New York into the 1950s.

    14. Isabelle Vengerova (1877–1956), Russian pianist and teacher, pupil of Theodor
Leschetizky, who came to the United States in 1923 and taught Barber from 1926 to
1931.

    15. Menotti told Fegley that Barber sometimes used him as an accompanist in recitals
where—just for fun—he was billed as John Carlo.

    16. Menotti told Fegley that Barber sang Brahms lieder for him.

GCM He had an enormous facility. He started composing when he was six years old, and by the time he was twelve or thirteen he was writing rather sophisticated pieces. He had a charming sense of humor, and some of the pieces he wrote in his teens are enchanting—some of the canons and rounds. I know that he didn't want to publish them, but now I feel it is my duty to do so.[17]

PD Did he write very easily?

GCM He was not a facile composer. I'm using the word "facility" because he was so gifted. He was a very tormented soul, never happy with what he had done. He was only happy while he was composing. Once he had finished the piece he could not bear to look at it. When he had to correct something, it was agony to go over a piece again. Also he suffered a great deal because he went through long periods of dryness—like Brahms or Rossini he sometimes went years without composing anything. Once he got into a piece, he would work day and night without stopping.

PD What sort of experiences drove his music?

GCM As you know, he has always been looked down on as a very traditional composer.

PD Not in those days?

GCM Even in those days. He was always considered apart. At that time the great innovator was supposed to be Copland, who had all the young people. Sam did not have a school and was considered old-fashioned. What bound us together so much was that we both believed in traditional values; he believed as deeply as I do that any human being and any artist must recognize a family—you are not born out of thin air. You have a father and a mother, and you might as well recognize that. . . . But he did not believe in being American. He has been accused of not being American enough, but Sam did not believe in nationalism, of having to be American in that sense. One had to be oneself. He said, "I don't feel particularly American." He always thought that one of the curses of Spanish music is that it is too Spanish. The poor Spanish composer has to be Spanish at all costs!

PD French composers did it better?

GCM French composers wrote Spanish music and nobody blamed them. They even wrote German music—even Debussy was influenced by Wagner. Sam never had that preoccupation of being American.

---

17. Very little has been published at the time of this writing.

PD   Before the war he might have been at a disadvantage because he wasn't
      obviously modern or obviously American. Copland said that it looked as
      if Barber ought to extend his style a bit. Later on he recognized that he
      had done so in the First Symphony and the Violin Concerto.[18] So, Barber
      was appreciated?

GCM   Yes, Sam was a very successful composer, especially with the audiences,
      but the critics have always been rather condescending toward his music.
      Yes, it is very well made but old-fashioned. There is always a "but." I feel
      rather bitter toward critics because now that he is dead, all of a sudden
      everybody's rediscovering Sam Barber. *The New York Times,* which so often
      damned his music, had his obituary on the first page. Immediately *Van-
      essa,* which was dropped by the major opera houses, is now going to be
      given at the New York City Opera, and there's some talk about the Metro-
      politan.[19] It's so sad that we all have to die [*laughs*] before anybody pays
      attention to us, and I feel it's the same thing with Sam.

PD   We've had a long run with new music being thrust at us, but aren't peo-
      ple now returning to the more traditional aspects?

GCM   That's part of the discovery, but I also feel that people have to recognize that
      he has left not only to American music but to the music of the century some
      works that are here to stay—for example, the Piano Sonata. I don't know a
      single piano sonata in the modern repertoire that has that strength and the
      power. I think some of his songs are here to remain: the Violin Concerto,
      the Piano Concerto. Very often I feel that some of his music at times sounds
      a bit manufactured. When he was uninspired you feel his music creaks a
      little bit. Even in the music of Brahms you feel the junctions when he has to
      go from one thing to another. He was not a Mendelssohnian composer with
      that flow—he had to work hard. But in certain works like the Piano Sonata,
      you don't feel that at all. His songs are very spontaneous.

18. Aaron Copland, *Copland on Music* (New York: Doubleday, 1960), 162: "Barber
writes in a somewhat outmoded fashion, making up in technical finish what he lacks in
musical substance. So excellent a craftsman should not content himself forever with the
emotionally conventional context of his present manner." Then Copland added a footnote: "Written when Barber was twenty-six. He must have arrived at a similar conclusion, if
one can judge by the sophisticated style of his more mature music."

19. *Vanessa* was premiered at the Met with thirteen performances in 1958–59; performed at the Spoleto Festival in 1961; again at the Met with five performances in 1965; at
Spoleto, Charleston, South Carolina, in 1978; as well as in many less prominent productions. Menotti confirmed to Fegley that he had put various things in the libretto of *Vanessa*
because Barber liked them and he knew they would inspire him. Leaving the house arises
from Chekhov's *The Cherry Orchard* (1904), one of Barber's favorite plays, at the end of
which he was always in tears—and it uncannily predicted the departure from Capricorn.

PD   The manufactured technique at this period suggests Hindemith.

GCM No, he did not like Hindemith. He said it was only technique with not much feeling, although he did like the couple of pieces we all like.

PD   *Mathis der Maler?*

GCM Yes. Actually, his musical loves changed. He started with Brahms, then he went through a certain influence of Sibelius. Then there was a period when he loved Chopin—I think until the end of his life. Then at the end, in the last years, he played only Bach. He had bought the *Gesellschaft* [edition]—that was his great love—and when he sat at the piano it was always to play some Bach.

PD   It's fascinating to focus on his influences at different stages. When he was interviewed in 1960, one of the scores on his piano was Schoenberg's Piano Concerto.[20]

Did he study that?

GCM He was very curious and was a very avid reader and did not ignore other currents of music. In a way I felt that was a bit damaging in his style because when you consider amplifying or modernizing one's style . . . I hate to consider bringing in my own convictions here, but in a way it's part of the conversation I often had with Sam. I feel that it's such a tragic thing that especially nowadays we consider art as a kind of industry. It's got to be bigger and better and more modern. Art doesn't change. A piece of pre-Colombian sculpture is no better or worse than a sculpture by Henry Moore. They are two different worlds, but art doesn't develop, doesn't change. The language may change, but we are not condemned to follow a trend of development in any way. In literature, where Thomas Mann wrote at the same time as James Joyce, people are free to write anything they want. Poetry is the same thing—we have Ezra Pound and we have Philip Larkin . . .

PD   Do you think that you had an effect on Barber's operas and vocal music?

GCM We always teased each other. He said I only wrote one good opera, my first one—*Amelia Goes to the Ball* [*laughs*]—and said, "I'm going to write a better opera than that!" I always encouraged him to write an opera because he wrote so beautifully for the voice, being a singer himself, and loved lieder. Although he was not particularly interested in opera, he had quite a good education in it because of his aunt, the famous contralto Louise Homer, who sang at the time of Caruso and was the leading contralto at

20. See Heyman, *Samuel Barber: The Composer and His Music*, 411.

the Metropolitan. So he heard all the operas as a child. He used to tell me that the only thing that interested him in opera was the noise of the mosquitoes in the third act of *Aida* [*laughs*] and the swan in *Lohengrin!*

But actually, through my operas he became more and more interested in dramatic music so that when he asked me to write a libretto for him I knew I could write the ideal libretto because I knew him so well and knew the things he loved. At that time he just finished reading the *Seven Gothic Tales* of Isak Dinesen, and he loved the book.[21] I thought it had the right atmosphere for Sam. He was a bit of a snob; he liked good food, he loved foreign countries. He loved northern countries and mystery, he had a bit of a gothic mind. So I set the opera in a northern country—I don't say what country because that would really spoil the fun for Sam— and with a castle. It starts with a menu with marvelous wines. He loved skating and was a wonderful skater, so there's a place when she goes skating. There's a doctor because Sam's father was a doctor, so I put that in. Then there was this quest for an ideal love that never seems to have come into Sam's life. The kind of love he would like to have had—love forever, eternal love that never changes. So that's the theme of the opera, this eternal waiting.

PD Ending in a kind of disillusion?

GCM Perhaps. Just in waiting.

PD Like that powerful piece called *The Lovers*. Was that a particular incident?

GCM I was not near him when he composed that.[22] I had already moved away from Capricorn, where we lived together for many years. At that time he had become a very difficult man, rude at times, very bitter—always with a marvelous sense of humor.

PD Vicious?

GCM Yes, but to the people he loved always a wonderful friend, very generous and thoughtful. It is extraordinary how, when he died, so many people to whom he had not been particularly kind suffered because of his death. It is marvelous the amount of letters I received mourning Sam's death. I was particularly moved by his hospital nurse. Sam was very sensitive to voices and could not bear an ugly voice or one with a vulgar accent. He couldn't stand that. During the last part of his illness the hospital sent

---

21. Baroness Karen von Blixen-Finecke (1885–1962); Danish writer also known as Isak Dinesen. *Seven Gothic Tales* (1934).

22. *The Lovers*, op. 43 (1971), was dedicated to Valentin Herranz, Barber's valet and final companion.

this Jewish girl from Brooklyn with a horrible voice! I cannot imitate it because I've had enough trouble with my own accent. [*laughs*] I cannot imitate anybody else's. The nurse herself told me that she came into the room and said, "Good evening, Mr. Barber, what can I do for you?" He didn't even open his eyes and said, "Yes, there is something you can do for me. Shut up!" So the nurse said, "That's not very kind, Mr. Barber." He replied, "Well, you asked me for a favor: I do not want to hear your voice, and keep away from me." She said, "I have to come near you because I have to clean you," and he said, "If you come near me and touch me, I'll bite you!" She did come near to clean him—at the time he couldn't move, poor thing—and he bit her! [*laughs*] And she bit him back! [*laughs*] Then he said, "You are a very stupid nurse." And she said, "You are a stupid composer. I may not know anything about composing, but you certainly don't know anything about nursing." They fought like that the whole night, and in the morning they were the best of friends and she was absolutely shattered when he died. Nurses don't easily cry, and she was crying like a baby. You had to break that shell. The first thing he did was resist friendship, he became very suspicious of any kind of affection for him. He wanted to protect himself.

PD   Did his personal friendships impinge on his music?

GCM   Oh yes, very much. He was a very emotional person. We shared the same house for many years, but then it became difficult for him to live in the country because I traveled so much. I had the festival in Spoleto and I had to stage my operas in France or wherever they were given. He was left alone for a long time and he could not bear to be alone, especially in the last part of his life. So I convinced him that the best thing would be for him to move to New York with an apartment and his own friends. He agreed to that. Then, when the house was sold and the time came for him to leave, he was really very shattered. I feel very guilty about Capricorn because I didn't realize how much it meant to him and what a terrible step it would be for him to move to New York.[23] After he moved, he got used to life in New York and loved his apartment, but in a certain way he always had this romantic feeling—he always mourned his youth and his youthful loves. He had this strange desire for some really romantic ideal. He loved German poetry—Hölderlin and Goethe—and spoke German quite well. He was akin to German romanticism.

---

23. In 2002 Geoffrey Norris went to see Menotti at Yester House and reported: "The relationship with Barber eventually faltered. It is something that clearly still touches Menotti deeply: tears well up in his eyes when he speaks of Barber dying in his arms." "The World's Favourite Opera Composer: Gian Carlo Menotti," *Daily Telegraph* (London), March 7, 2002.

PD This aspect is sometimes discussed as a kind of innocence and nostalgia, as in *Knoxville*. Is that what it was?

GCM He had a great *sehnsucht* for his childhood in West Chester. In that way he was very American, but the America he loved was very different from that of Copland. He didn't care about the Midwest or California and was a New Englander. In a certain way, that tied him to Europe. He loved the English heritage that went to America through New England and felt that the rest was fake America.

PD He had this polished background. Not only the celebrated opera singer Louise Homer, but her husband, Sydney, was a composer. Do you know his songs?

GCM Yes, and some of them are lovely. I met them both. Sam had a great love of the countryside around his home in Pennsylvania. It's a kind of America that very few foreigners know. I was brought up there [from the age of seventeen], so I know it quite well.

PD Did he actually hate the folksy Americana of Copland and Harris?

GCM Yes, absolutely. He refused to touch it! [*laughs*] As a matter of fact, he did not even like Ives. He always told me: "To be American that way is much too easy—just like somebody who paints palm trees thinks he's become an African! A collage of a little bit of this and that doesn't make American music American."

PD I'm not going to pick up on Ives because I know you don't like him either.

GCM No [*laughs*]—a *pasticcióne!*[24]

PD It was fashionable for American composers of MacDowell's generation to have European sources, and the serialists after World War II adopted an international idiom, so why was Barber's generation expected to be overtly American?

GCM Thank God I'm not a musicologist! [*laughs*] Don't try to make me one! [*laughs*]

Going back to Sam's joys and sorrows, one thing that was a terrible blow was the failure of *Antony and Cleopatra* at the Met.[25] He never quite got

---

24. A busybody, meddler, or pasticheur. In 1979 Barber told Philip Ramey: "I can't bear Ives. It is now unfashionable to say this, but in my opinion he was an amateur, a hack, who didn't put pieces together well." Cited in Heyman, *Samuel Barber: The Composer and His Music*, 232.

25. 16 September 1966: see interviews with Leontyne Price, John Browning, and others here.

over that. Not so much because the opera was not a success, but he received such vitriolic reviews from all over the world. They spared him nothing. Even now, when they talk about his life they always mention the terrible flop—God knows every composer has flops, but somehow nobody has forgiven Sam for *Antony and Cleopatra*.[26]

PD   But it's not that bad, since you did the revival at Juilliard in 1974?

GCM   The revival was immensely successful, with some beautiful music, and the opera now works. I helped him, but perhaps the only moment of bitterness that ever existed between us was because of *Antony and Cleopatra*. When he was asked to write the second opera all his friends said: "Oh, don't do it again with Gian Carlo. You're not sharing the same house; you're not even together now." He let himself be convinced, and I was very hurt by that. I was dying to write another libretto for Sam: it would have been a joy. In a certain way, part of the trouble was that Franco Zeffirelli did not understand Sam's character and filled the libretto with fanfares and big scenes and so on. Sam has always been a very intimate and introverted composer, and all that was completely out of style. When we did the revision he was like a child. He would say: "What do you want to do with it? Do I have to throw away the whole thing?" I said, "No." He cut most of the fanfares and the part that was unconvincing. Then he added a very beautiful love duet, which was needed because there was very little love originally.

PD   But wasn't the original failure because of the epic spectacular occasion of the premiere of the opening of the Lincoln Center putting the music under colossal pressure?

GCM   Very much so. But I must say the opera was not well constructed. It was about death and pomp, and there was very little love in it. Once I pointed that out to Sam, he developed the more lyrical part. Now I think it is perhaps not as strong as *Vanessa,* but it is a very valid work. The Juilliard revival was [such] a tremendous success that they had to repeat [it] in a second season, and there are plans for Spoleto.[27]

PD   Barber came to opera relatively late. Is the essence of his music in opera, the concertos, or the songs?

---

26. Menotti confirmed to Fegley, "That was really the beginning of the decline in his health and he suffered very much."

27. *Antony and Cleopatra* was put on jointly by the Spoleto Festival USA and the Festival of Two Worlds in June 1983. It was recorded live at Spoleto, Italy, for New World Records, NW 322/323/324.

GCM That's very difficult, but I would say that the Sam that touches me most is in the songs. Some are absolutely exquisite, but also the last act of *Vanessa* still moves me to tears. Perhaps because it's tied to so many memories. It's a marvelous work. If you think that so many operas live only because they have about two good arias [*laughs*], it's really wonderful to have an opera that works from the first note to the last. At the memorial concert we played almost half of the last act with piano and voices—John Browning playing—and everybody was terribly moved. It comes over even without the orchestra.

Talking about the funeral, I want to tell you something that may be amusing. He had a wonderful sense of humor, and he loved to shock people with unconventional phrases and actions. He loved good food, and one of his favorite things was a good soup with French croutons sprinkled on. He said: "When I die, please remember I don't want flowers, I just want croutons. Get a sack of croutons and sprinkle them over my coffin." That we did. Some friends of his baked some bread and made some croutons. I didn't have the courage to do it, but as his coffin was lowered three of his friends sprinkled croutons. I could just see Sam laughing.[28] [*laughs*]

PD Wasn't the *Adagio for Strings* performed in the hospital?

GCM It was very moving, and there was a movement of the sonata and a couple of songs. I don't know how much he took in, but he listened and at the end said "thank you: beautiful." He could speak very little at that time. He was a little bit bored by the *Adagio for Strings* [*laughs*], always haunted by it.

---

28. On November 24, 1981, Fegley interviewed Frances T. Herron in West Chester. She told him about the funeral at Oaklands Cemetery: "Our minister told me that Gian Carlo did a strange thing. He threw bread cubes on the casket . . . and said it was an old Italian custom to throw bread cubes instead of dirt after the casket is lowered." Herron thought Gian Carlo might have been joking but said he was very concerned about all the arrangements: "If he called him once, he called the minister twenty-one times about the details." However, Lee Hoiby, who was at the funeral, told Pierre Brévignon that Valentin Herranz was the only person to throw croutons and that it angered Menotti. (E-mail from Brévignon to me, July 20, 2009.) Those attending the funeral were mostly New Yorkers because Barber had not been seen in West Chester since his mother's death in 1967. Barber's request to have croutons thrown over his grave dates back; see Broder, *Samuel Barber*, 46. Menotti told Fegley in 1981 that Barber had wanted to be buried in West Chester and that there was "a plot for me right next to his grave." Menotti was buried instead at Yester House, Gifford, East Lothian, Scotland—letter from Francis Menotti, February 26, 2007—but there is a stone inscribed "To the Memory of Two Friends" on the plot next to Barber's grave in West Chester. Yester House is the imposing stone mansion in a five-hundred-acre estate, built between 1699 and 1728 by James Smith and Alexander McGill with modifications and interiors by William and Robert Adam. It was offered for sale in 2008.

PD   Do you remember the *Adagio* in the String Quartet?

GCM   He was not particularly fond of the String Quartet, but he did like the *Adagio* and decided to orchestrate it. He wrote it in Austria at St. Wolfgang.

PD   Did he mind that it became the most famous piece of American orchestral music?

GCM   He did mind that it was always played at funerals! [*laughs*]. As a matter of fact, I was very careful not to have it played at his funeral because I knew he'd rather have the croutons [*laughs*] than the *Adagio for Strings!* He liked the piece but thought he had written much better music than that.

When he talked about my own music, he always made two very valid criticisms. I don't mind criticism when it hits the spot, and he was a severe critic. He said, "Your music lacks ample breathing; it's made of short breathing." It's true, and I'm trying in my later work to develop a longer line. Sam had big lungs in his music. He had the lovely lyric sense that expanded into long lines—it was not the anxious breathing like my own. [*laughs*] I'm always running! He also had a great sense of form, one of the things that often stopped him in his composing because he'd always see the piece as a huge construction. I jump into my piece sometimes just as when a child I would jump into cold water—just close my eyes and pray to God. But he had to see the whole construction in front of his eyes first.

The other thing that he always criticized in my music was quite valid but cannot be applied to him. He said: "You don't move your basses. Most of your music is built on pedal notes. I can just hum one note, you can put anything on top, and anything goes."

That, I think, is an important criticism to most contemporary music. Sam was very conscious of that, and that's why his music works so beautifully, and he had a wonderful contrapuntal sense.

PD   And a good harmonic sense too? As in the slow movement of the Piano Concerto.

GCM   And the quintet in *Vanessa.*

PD   Did he have an acute ear? A sense of orchestral sonority?

GCM   Well, if I may be completely candid about that—and I'm sure Sam would forgive me—I never thought he was a great orchestrator. I don't think he was that interested in orchestration. It's just serviceable for his music, but it doesn't add anything. It's not like Ravel or Prokofiev. I don't feel Sam's soul in the style of orchestration. He often said: "The color of the orchestra doesn't really interest me that much because I feel that the musical values should remain the same whatever instrument is used. The orchestra in a hundred years will be completely different, and then what will happen to all those wonderful sounds of Debussy and Ravel and so on."

He said: "Look at Bach. You play it on the harmonica, the guitar, or the organ. It's always wonderful."

PD   That's why he could transcribe *Souvenirs* from piano duet to orchestra and the *Agnus Dei* from the *Adagio?*

GCM   Those he did, frankly, just to make money. We sign off our compositions to a publisher. There were so many requests that, rather than let somebody else do it, he did it himself. In those moments of dryness—just to do something.

PD   Just commercial?

GCM   As a matter of fact, I didn't know the transcription of the *Adagio for Strings* existed until somebody brought it to me. I was horrified! [*laughs*]

PD   It's published in the *Complete Choral Music.*[29]

GCM   I know. It shouldn't be there.[30]

PD   Is it something to do with the tunes that makes Barber's personality? Their memorability? You understand that in your own music.

GCM   I don't like to call those "tunes" because I think I'm using thematic material. A good theme is not always a tune. But then again—for God's sake—you're making me talk about things that are so difficult to explain. What is a tune and what is a good theme? Nobody can explain it. I always feel, with James Joyce, that "art is a form of memory." A beautiful melody is a form of memory. Let us say the collective unconscious, something that we all know even before it has been done. How can we explain [*sings the first phrase of the Barcarolle from Offenbach's* The Tales of Hoffmann] the three notes that make a melody? If you go [*sings the same notes, changing the order*], this is not a melody. Why? Those three notes bring back a memory of God knows what. I think that Sam has the sense of the inevitable in his music, like a discovery . . .

PD   The good Broadway composer, such as Gershwin, has to have memorability, and Barber has some of that?

---

29. New York: G. Schirmer, 1979.

30. This now seems like a surprising reaction to what has become a popular choral piece, with thirty-five different recordings in the catalog in 2008.

GCM I think it's very important. The greatness of a composer like Schubert, Beethoven, Mozart. Can you explain the impact of the repeated notes at the beginning of the *Moonlight Sonata* played every year all over the world? Impossible. But everybody who hears that phrase remembers it.

PD How often did you show each other your compositions?

GCM All through our lives; we always did.

PD At what stage would he show you pieces?

GCM Generally, when it was finished. Sometimes he would play me the very beginning and would ask me whether it was worth going on or not. He might say, "I think I should throw it away." And you knew that you had to say, "Oh, marvelous!" He had to have that, like a little ceremony. Then he would show it to me when it was finished.[31]

PD Did he write for particular performers? For example, did Horowitz have an impact on the Piano Sonata?

GCM Oh yes, definitely. He liked Horowitz's playing very much and was very happy when he asked him to write the sonata for him. He worked quite closely with Horowitz. When he'd finished the first movement, he came to Capricorn and played [it] and suggested a few technical changes. Horowitz did ask him to write a very difficult sonata and to make it something very challenging. Heaven knows he did: I certainly couldn't play it! [*laughs*] When it was done, everybody thought the last movement was a tremendous challenge—now all these young pianists seem to be able to play anything at all.

PD Curiously enough, there's a fugue in the Elliott Carter sonata, rather a different composer?[32]

GCM The challenge of form is creeping back into music. Everybody feels they've had enough freedom for a while. Now they want to lock the bird into a cage.

PD How were things organized at Capricorn?

GCM Capricorn was a rather curious house. We wanted something that had two very separate wings with studios far enough away so we couldn't hear each other compose or play the piano. We looked at countless houses

---

31. Menotti told Fegley that Barber was reluctant to go over old works and needed to be encouraged: "I helped him a great deal because I would make him rewrite things, would egg him on and torment him until he really had made at least some of the changes."

32. There are fugues at the end of three major American piano sonatas—those by Charles Tomlinson Griffes (1918), Carter (1946), and Barber (1949).

when we decided to buy a house together. If we liked the house, Sam would go to one corner of the house, I would go to the other, and we would scream at each other and sing very loudly—in the horrified presence of the agent or the owner! They couldn't understand what was going on. Then we would come in to say no, thank you, and not bother looking at the rest of the house. Finally we found this strange house, which looked very much like a Swedish chalet, and we actually could not hear each other.

With the help of friends, we were able to buy the house.[33] It became quite famous because we had very intense weekends; practically all the New York intellectuals came through Capricorn at one time or another. Not only musicians but mainly writers and painters. People you would never think would be our friends, like Duchamp and Andy Warhol.[34] [*laughs*] Actually, Warhol was a great friend of Sam's for some time; he designed the cover for *A Hand of Bridge,* for which I wrote the libretto.[35] They used to kid around an awful lot. Once they went to a restaurant in New York and were laughing so loud with so many terrible jokes that they were both thrown out of the restaurant! [*laughs*] Then Sam thought people were taking Warhol too seriously. Sam was always very much interested in painting and in literature. Most of his friends were writers, poets, and painters rather than musicians.

PD   Close to a French tradition perhaps, and something of Poulenc comes through in the *Melodies passagères?*

GCM   He was a great friend of Poulenc, who often came to Capricorn with Bernac. I would say that he was probably the only composer that was very near Sam.

PD   Really?

GCM   I cannot think of anybody else. Of the well-known composers, he was probably the only one who seemed to love Sam's music and to be near him. Although I knew Poulenc quite well myself, he was Sam's friend more than mine.

PD   Did he possess much of Poulenc's music?

---

33. The house was acquired in 1943 with the help of Mary Curtis Bok. Barber and Menotti shared it until 1973.

34. Marcel Duchamp (1887–1968), revolutionary French-born avant-garde artist and theorist; Andy Warhol (1928–87), influential American artist and celebrity who pioneered pop art.

35. *A Hand of Bridge,* op. 35 (1959), a mini-opera with libretto by Menotti for four soloists and chamber orchestra lasting nine minutes.

GCM Oh yes. He had a marvelous library.

PD What other contemporary composers?

GCM Stravinsky, of course; quite a bit of Benjamin Britten; he studied Berg and Schoenberg, was curious about them but never really liked them. He always predicted that Poulenc's songs, within twentieth-century music, would be the most durable, although now everybody considers them light. But I think his prediction was a valid one.

PD Presumably, he was interested in twelve-tone techniques after Copland and Stravinsky went that way around 1950?

GCM He did study twelve-tone techniques but was never interested at all in electronic music. That bored him absolutely completely.

PD If you had one piece to choose . . .

GCM Oh no, don't ask me that! [*laughs*] It's like being on *Desert Island Discs!*

I would like to say that not only was he very much interested in literature, but he himself was a very charming writer. I am planning to publish some of his letters, especially those he wrote in his twenties.[36]

[In his interview with Brent Fegley, Menotti summed up: "It's funny that we were such wonderful friends and had such a wonderful life together. I loved gambling; he hated it. I loved playing cards; he never learned to play and to the end of his life he didn't know the difference between a club and a diamond. He was poor at sports because he had bad eyesight, but he was a good swimmer and skier. I tried desperately to interest him in tennis, my favorite sport, but that was absolutely hopeless. He never watched football or baseball: anything like that was just a complete bore to him. . . .[37] But we loved the same books, we loved to go to museums to look at the pictures, we loved to go to the theater, but he was never really interested in films. We loved to travel: he had friends all over the world."]

---

36. Menotti told Fegley that Barber was "a beautiful letter writer." He wrote to Mary Curtis Bok from abroad, but those letters were destroyed by her heirs.

37. In 1931 Barber very much enjoyed playing tennis and even told his parents that he enjoyed it more than his musical studies. Heyman, *Samuel Barber: The Composer and His Music,* 82, 89.

Chapter Seven

Charles Turner

Interview with Peter Dickinson, New York City, May 13, 1981

Introduction

Charles Turner (1928–2003), composer and teacher based in New York, was introduced to Barber by Gore Vidal in 1950 and soon became part of the entourage at Capricorn. Barber, Menotti, and Turner, along with the conductor Thomas Schippers, shared summer retreats in Maine and Italy.[1] Turner was also a violinist who performed the Violin Concerto under Barber's baton in Germany in 1951, to the composer's great satisfaction. *Souvenirs* was dedicated to Turner, and Barber entrusted the score of his final work, Canzonetta for Oboe and Strings, to him to orchestrate.

I met Turner again in New York in 1990, and in a subsequent letter he gave me some of his own background: "My first orchestral work in 1956 [probably *Encounter*] was played by Szell, Reiner, Mitropolous and Schippers, in that order, and another work was played by Schippers at the Philharmonic in 1964. A ballet commissioned by Lincoln Kirstein had success and many performances by all the major companies for ten years and was revived last year and called a masterpiece by some critics [*Dark Pastorale*, choreographed by Francisco Moncion; see *The New York Times*, February 15, 1957]. I have taught harmony, counterpoint, orchestration, all those composition things, for forty years and every week some former student's work appears here.[2] This week it is John Zorn with a Kronos Quartet commission.[3] I studied with Barber for five years—Boulanger before

---

1. John Gruen, *Menotti: A Biography* (New York: Macmillan, 1978), 104–7.
2. Turner wrote music for a school production of *The Ballad of Barnaby* (1969), a drama by W. H. Auden.
3. John Zorn (1953–), American composer and saxophonist, attended the United Nations School as a child where he was taught by Turner and Leonardo Balada.

that—and I am the only pupil he ever put through the same training he got from Scalero at Curtis."[4]

Earlier, after I had sent him a copy of the BBC Radio 3 documentary based on the interviews in this book, Turner wrote: "I think you did a splendid job. It is so sensitively and intelligently done and gives such a good picture of Sam and his music. The most clear-eyed speakers were Copland, Schuman and Hitchcock, I thought. Menotti romanticized and distorted a little, and so did Browning, but they always do, and that too is interesting. I liked the Rashomon quality you got at times. Do you remember that Japanese film in which three people who have seen the same thing describe it differently?"[5]

Interview

PD   What was Samuel Barber like?

CT   Well, he was a very witty man. His wit is rather hard to capture. He kept us all amused with his funny remarks. When I first met him in 1950 I thought he was one of the most brilliant speakers I'd ever met. He could be dazzling at a party and hold forth and say all sorts of brilliant things. Not just about music. He read a great deal, and he was perfectly at home in Italian and French. He spoke three languages every day of his life and he always had servants who did that. The Spanish servant who was with him the last ten years of his life spoke those languages too.[6] That's a little unusual for an American unless he lives in Europe part of the time—which Sam did.

We sometimes say he was a bit on the mean side because he said things to us that were so frank that they hurt a little bit. Finally, that was one of his charms. He always told his friends what he thought of them. In the long run, we didn't mind.

PD   Are there any incidents you recall?

---

4. Letter of November 28, 1990. Natasha Litvin, pianist, writer, and widow of Sir Stephen Spender, knew the scene at Capricorn; they both visited regularly when he was at Sarah Lawrence College in 1947–48. She remembered that Barber and Menotti appeared to be pushing Turner to be a composer, which seemed unfair. The scene at Capricorn was always very busy, with both composers working furiously on something, but they still had time to prepare spoof soap operas for entertainment. Telephone conversation, June 30, 2009.

5. Letter of April 9, 1982.

6. Valentin Herranz (1944–) was employed by Barber as a valet and companion for the last decade of his life.

CT   When he was dying in the hospital lots of his old friends came to see him, but one person with whom he'd been very friendly years ago hadn't been to see him or called him up for years and was presumably mad at him. Somebody said, "Have you heard from Henri-Louis?" and Sam said, "Oh yes, he sent me a thousand roses!"[7]

He loved to make funny remarks at other people's expense—but only in private.

PD   What's immediately recognizable about him and his music?

CT   The Italian influence in his life was very strong. His teacher—Scalero—was Italian; his best friend was an Italian composer—Menotti; and he went to Italy every year of his life and owned a house there. Many Americans went to study with Boulanger, but he didn't—he was Italian in that sense and therefore lyrical and vocal in inspiration. He was an excellent singer himself.

PD   Were there tensions in his life that emerge in the dramatic intensity of some of his works?

CT   Sam was very outspoken and a good deal more emotional than I suppose many American and English people are. He met Menotti in his teens, and I think they both decided they were going to be successful composers—and they certainly were. It wasn't a competition but two good friends who were doing the same sort of thing—helping each other.

PD   Menotti seems to think there was a bit of jealousy over the great success of his operas.

CT   Sam was a jealous person about all his friends but especially about Menotti. When Menotti became very famous after *The Consul* (1950) was done, the house was often filled with his staff, his singers, his friends or reporters, and Sam didn't like that very much sometimes.

PD   Are there musical influences from Menotti?

CT   More the other way, probably. I think the chief musical influences on Sam were dead composers like Bach. Especially when he was getting ready to write a new piece he'd play a lot of Bach. Sometimes Chopin, but you can hear the influence of Bach. I don't think they influenced each other particularly. They helped each other a great deal. Gian Carlo was a wonderful friend to Sam's operas; when nobody else was producing them, he did. He produced *Vanessa* at Spoleto and Charleston and

---

7. Henri-Louis de la Grange (1924–), leading authority on Mahler, Honorary Founder and president of the Médiathèque Musicale Mahler, Paris.

directed *Antony and Cleopatra* at Juilliard wonderfully well. He got *Vanessa* televised—that was a generous thing to do for a famous opera composer.

PD   Would Barber have turned to opera without Menotti?

CT   I don't know. People wanted him to write operas before that. The libretto of *Vanessa* was tailor-made for him, with little details specially for Sam. Things like the man who borrows a comb—Sam never had a comb and always had to borrow one. And Sam loved being read aloud to—that's why that's in there, I suppose. The waltz, too; that's the kind of dancing he liked. He liked to waltz, the only kind of dancing I knew him to do.

PD   And *Souvenirs,* written for you, has waltzes?[8]

CT   That was written after the Piano Sonata—a great success and one of his best pieces, I think. He couldn't compose anything for a long time after that. I happened to meet him during that period and he said, "When I look at the music paper I feel frightened. I can't think of anything." So I said, "Why don't you write a party piece, something we can play at parties?" And so he wrote *Souvenirs*.

He used to go to a bar sometimes called the Blue Angel—I don't know that it exists anymore—and there were two people, Edie and Rack, who played rather sophisticated cabaret music on two pianos. *Souvenirs* was a little bit in that café mood. We did play it at parties all over Europe.

PD   What are Barber's most enduring pieces?

CT   I think the operas are awfully good. The public doesn't seem to agree with me yet, but I think they may someday. *Knoxville* certainly is a wonderful piece. So is the Cello Concerto and that hasn't been played very much. I like those early pieces with English titles like *School for Scandal, Scenes from Shelley,* and *Dover Beach*.

PD   Is there anything particularly American about his music?

CT   I think there is in *Knoxville*. We Americans fall apart when we hear that. It's so much like our family life—different from England, more sentimental possibly. But that's the way we are.

PD   It's a kind of nostalgia?

CT   We talk a lot about loving each other. English people wouldn't. [*laughs*] It isn't that they don't love each other, but they just wouldn't talk about it! We do. Sam's own family were close to him and he liked them. I didn't

---

8. *Souvenirs,* op. 28 (1952), for piano duet, ballet choreographed by Todd Bolender at New York City Ballet, November 15, 1955, and very favorably received.

meet most of them, but I know he had five aunts whom he adored. Gian Carlo knew them too. One was the famous singer Louise Homer; the others were people he was close to and they had family jokes that seem a bit naïve, I suppose, but they were charming. He adored his sister, and when she died he was very upset for a long time. And he loved his parents. So all that feeling in *Knoxville* is very real.

He was very nice to his nephews, and when they wanted to come to New York he always treated them—gave them the best time he could.

PD   Why was the *Adagio* such a smash hit?

CT   Possibly it's about death, that piece, I'm not sure. Its mood is elegiac. When he died—and I saw quite a lot of him in his last years—I watched him and so did everyone, and his nurse said, "I've never seen anyone die with so much class or surrounded with so much love." He was very brave—it wasn't an easy time the last year. He never complained but kept making jokes all the time.

PD   What happened at the funeral?

CT   That's one of the jokes. His family had jokes about cemeteries and dying. I suppose they were a little bit childish, but I remember him making a joke with his mother that when he died he didn't want to be buried next to Uncle Will because his hair was parted in the middle. He wanted a tree planted at his head because he didn't like the sun shining in his eyes. I thought this was rather frivolous when I first heard it but later thought it was charming. When he was buried in the cemetery, croutons were thrown on his coffin because he always asked for that. Then his servant Valentino threw a packet of cigarettes because he promised to give up smoking when Sam died. This was a gesture of good intention.

PD   Can I bring you back to the *Adagio?*

CT   It's really our national funeral piece. I think it's been played when anybody of importance has died since Franklin Roosevelt. When Kennedy was shot, it was on the radio ten minutes after he died.

There was a party given for Sam a week before he died in which a string quartet played the *Adagio*. This was a very difficult scene for me because it was like being at Sam's funeral while he was still alive.

AJ   What was life like at Capricorn?

CT   It was ideal for two composers because at each end of the house there was a studio where Sam and Gian Carlo could work without hearing each other. They had a brilliant social life going on too—not with the neighbors but with artists who came to see them. Sometimes just for a meal—

it's only an hour out from New York—or for a weekend. Menotti was a wonderful host who loved having people around him. The people who came were fascinating very often. All sorts, not just musicians but actors and writers. It was a place people wanted to be invited to because they knew it was something special. Sam would be brilliant—more lemony than Gian Carlo, who was warm, hospitable, and kindly in his manner. Not that Sam wasn't too, but he loved to make naughty remarks. I don't mean off-color remarks—he never did that and he didn't like it—but just telling people what he thought of them when it wasn't necessarily complimentary. The one he did this most of all to was Gian Carlo. When I first went I was rather shocked at the things he said to him, but Gian Carlo didn't seem to mind and took it all in his stride.

The house had to be in good order at all times. It had to look in good condition too; nothing could be run down. He once came and stayed here with me, and the wallpaper was coming off in the bathroom. He said, "I can't take a bath in a bathroom where the wallpaper's coming off." He was that fussy! [*laughs*]

PD How did he adjust to being conservative when the fashion was for the avant-garde?

CT I think he had a pretty lonely time of it sometimes because he was trying to write music that wasn't fashionable in terms of what most composers were doing. I suspect that's one of the reasons he and Menotti remained friends so long because Menotti supported him in all this. I think it took a certain amount of courage for him to do it. He was very sensitive to criticism. You weren't allowed to talk about reviews at all, especially if they were bad. He didn't have any close friends who were critics. I don't know what he really felt, but he didn't want to see them very often. He thought it was all right if they did their job, but he didn't want to know anything about it. He protected himself by not reading the reviews.[9]

PD There have been some savage things said about both Barber and Menotti.

CT Yes, of course. Virgil Thomson told me Sam has been number one on the charts for years. I think the public gets the impression that Copland was because he's been in the public eye and Sam wasn't. But posterity has already spoken.

He didn't do anything to further his career in the last fifteen years of his life, nothing I knew about. He never pursued conductors or

---

9. But see Barber's interview with Robert Sherman, chapter 4.

performers. They pursued him sometimes. Pianists especially who hoped they'd get another sonata or concerto out of him—but they didn't. The period when I studied with him was in the 1950s when he wrote *Vanessa, Summer Music,* and then the Piano Concerto. I think *Vanessa* is marvelous, but the Piano Concerto has a kind of assurance and authority on a grand scale that doesn't really happen before that. When I was studying with Sam I used to try to be a bit contemporary and write things in 5/8 or 5/4. Sam would say: "You're always bringing these things in five—why do you do that? I'm so bored with it." But the last movement of the Piano Concerto is entirely in 5/8, and he wrote it the week before the first performance! He couldn't think of anything and suddenly got going. It was a clinching movement, very exciting. John Browning was sensationally successful with it.

1. Samuel Barber on the steps of his garden studio in Rome, 1935. (Copyright G. Schirmer Archives; reprinted by permission.)

2. Samuel Barber in army uniform, c. 1942. (Copyright G. Schirmer Archives; reprinted by permission.)

3. Samuel Barber and Mary Louise Bok Zimbalist, the founder of Curtis, leaving for vacation in Bermuda, 1947. (Copyright G. Schirmer Archives; reprinted by permission.)

4. Samuel Barber outside Capricorn, his Mt. Kisco Home, 1948. (Copyright G. Schirmer Archives; reprinted by permission.)

5. Samuel Barber standing beside his record player, 1940s. (Copyright G. Schirmer Archives; reprinted by permission.)

6. Samuel Barber in his studio at the American Academy in Rome, 1953. (Copyright G. Schirmer Archives; reprinted by permission.)

7. Samuel Barber, Gian Carlo Menotti, and Eleanor Steber (in costume as Vanessa), January 1958. (Copyright G. Schirmer Archives; reprinted by permission.)

8. Samuel Barber and Gian Carlo Menotti, with score of *Vanessa*, 1958. (Copyright G. Schirmer Archives; reprinted by permission.)

9. Samuel Barber and John Browning, discussing Barber's Concerto for Piano and Orchestra, before premiere with Boston Symphony, September 1962. (Copyright G. Schirmer Archives; reprinted by permission.)

10. Samuel Barber, photo inscribed to Robert White, 1978. (Copyright G. Schirmer Archives; reprinted by permission.)

11. Samuel Barber's grave, Oaklands Cemetery, West Chester, Pennsylvania. (Photo taken by Ulrich Klabunde; reprinted by permission.)

Part Four

Composers

Chapter Eight

Aaron Copland

Interview with Peter Dickinson, Rock Hill, Peekskill, NY, May 11, 1981

Introduction

Aaron Copland (1900–1990) needs no introduction as a leading figure in American music from the late 1920s until his death. Along with Gershwin and Bernstein, he has exemplified American music on the international scene for over half a century.[1] He lacked Gershwin's spectacular appeal based on popular song and musical theater, and he could not compete with Bernstein's extravagant public career as conductor, composer, and pianist. But Copland, who took up conducting after Koussevitsky's death in 1951, became a much-loved figure on the podium, with an international following. He wrote for films and reached a wide audience through television.

Unlike Barber, he was adept at musical politics. He knew how to get things done through patrons and organizations and worked hard to support colleagues. His writings were designed to inform listeners and to put forth the case for American music.

Copland stopped composing in the early 1970s but continued his conducting career for another decade. His last European trip was in 1980. He gave a concert with the London Symphony Orchestra at the Royal Festival Hall on December 2, and the next day he was interviewed by Anthony Burton at the United States Embassy. When he said three times that he had never heard of Nadia Boulanger before he went to Paris, it was clear that Alzheimer's disease

---

1. Copland valued his connections with the UK where he was a regular visitor, later as a conductor. A British perspective emerges from his obituaries: *The Times*, December 4, 1990; Hugo Cole and Meirion Bowen in the *Guardian*, December 4, 1990; and Bayan Northcott, Peter Dickinson, and Malcolm Williamson in the *Independent*, December 4, 1990. See also Peter Dickinson, ed., *Copland Connotations: Studies and Interviews* (Woodbridge, Suffolk: Boydell, 2002).

was starting to impact his final years. There is some evidence of this in the interview that follows, which has been compressed to avoid repetition, although the points he made have characteristic authority. During the 1980s Copland wound down slowly at home, receiving many honors and supported by friends. He collaborated with Vivian Perlis on his memoirs, an essential portrayal of the life and work of a unique man and musician.[2]

In *Music and Imagination,* Copland's Harvard lectures delivered in 1951–52, his chapter "Musical Imagination in the Americas" argues for a distinctively American music of the kind that brought him to a wide public in the 1930s, but he generously recognizes that there is another side to the question: "Roger Sessions, Walter Piston and Samuel Barber are composers whose works are not strikingly American . . . and yet a full summary of the American imagination at work in music . . . would naturally stress the import of their work. There is a universalist ideal, exemplified by their symphonies and chamber music, that belittles the nationalistic note and stresses predominantly musical values."[3]

Arthur Johnson and I arrived at Copland's house in the woods in continuous heavy rain. When we settled down to record the interview, it looked as though Copland had his copy of *Music in a New Found Land* by Wilfrid Mellers accessible, so our talk opened with that.[4]

Interview

By Permission of the Aaron Copland Fund

AC   Did you ever happen to read about Sam Barber in this particular book?

PD   Yes—it's about one of the best discussions.

AC   Of course it is.

PD   As is the section on you. He does a very good job.

AC   He's a brilliant writer, Mellers, a brilliant man.

I must explain to you that while I knew Barber over the years, we were never very close as friends. We were fellow composers. But I was considered to be much more *moderne* than he was. From where I sat, Sam was

---

2. Aaron Copland and Vivian Perlis, *Copland: 1900 through 1942* (New York: St. Martin's, 1984); Copland and Perlis, *Copland since 1943* (New York: St. Martin's, 1989).

3. Aaron Copland, *Music and Imagination* (Cambridge: Harvard University Press, 1952), 94–94.

4. Wilfrid Mellers (1914–2008), British writer, teacher, and composer. He founded the Music Department at York University in 1964, and his *Music in a New Found Land* (London: Barrie and Rockcliff, 1964) was a ground-breaking study of American music.

rather conservative in his musical style, and so what he was writing at that
time lacked a kind of excitement. We were all looking for new things à la
Stravinsky and Schoenberg. But in retrospect, of course, it looks different. I mean, it doesn't matter any more that Sam wasn't right up there in
the front of the modernists doing things that were very controversial, as
in my own case. Of course, people forget that when I was in my mid-twen-
ties I was lambasted by the press as a wild-eyed modernist. Sam never had
that kind of experience at all.

He wrote music that was very acceptable, in its quiet moods very touching
and very well done. That was always a pleasure. You knew in advance that
if you were going to hear a new piece of Samuel Barber it would make
sense; it would be understandable even on a first hearing. It just seemed
solid, good work without being what we were all interested in—and that
would be the far-out idiom, the things Stravinsky and Schoenberg were
doing. It's possible that Stravinsky interested him more than Schoenberg.

PD   You say it didn't matter that Barber was a conservative composer, so what
      are his most enduring pieces?

AC   I'm not sure that I'm in a good position to tell you that since I haven't
      been so closely associated that I know or have even heard everything
      he wrote. I know the general style of his music, and I'd be surprised if I
      didn't recognize a piece as being his. But we were living in two different
      musical worlds. I was allied more with the far-out people in New York—
      the League of Composers.[5] By comparison I thought of Sam as not so
      interested in the latest thing but always writing his music from an inner
      need that did not take a revolutionary turn at all. It was what a composer
      perhaps of fifty years ago might have felt. I don't think he was at all inter-
      ested in writing rhythms that nobody else had dreamt up. I had that kind
      of yen at the time, whether it was carried out or not. He seemed almost
      too safe, so that I wasn't as aware of the music he was writing as I later
      became over the years.

PD   But you must have seen a piece like the *Adagio for Strings* become a classic
      of an almost enviable kind?

AC   Yes, of course I was aware of that. Sure. But it wasn't breaking any new
      paths, creating harmonies we'd never heard before. It was very felt,
      coming right out of the insides of him. The things he felt like doing he

---

5. The League of Composers was founded in New York in 1923 following disagreements within the International Composers Guild. The league commissioned works, ran
the journal *Modern Music*, and put on concerts including significant American premieres
of pieces by major European composers. Copland was executive chairman from 1948 to
1950. See Carol J. Oja, *Making Music Modern* (New York: Oxford University Press, 2000).

did very effectively, so it was convincing and I think it will stand up like really first-class music.

PD   Is his music American?

AC   I'm not sure I'd be able to recognize it as American. I don't think he had any conscious desire to write music that was immediately recognizable as American. That made him somewhat different. He could have been quite at home living in England or any other place around the world, while we were very intent—some of us—on expressing an American quality in our concert music such as our jazz composers had been able to do so successfully. I don't think he had any interest in that kind of thing.

PD   Does it matter?

AC   It seemed to matter at the time since [*laughs*] he wasn't joining the crowd—the other composers—and was living a well-settled life. Not taking the chances that we were taking rhythmically, for example; I don't think you'll find his music full of 7/8s and 9/16ths and things that caused interpretative problems.

PD   Can I press you to suggest pieces that represent him best?

AC   Of course the *Adagio for Strings* comes to mind, but that's one comparatively short piece. I think the operas were the most ambitious thing he ever did. I'm ashamed to say I never actually saw one full opera, but I've heard excerpts.

PD   Why is the *Adagio* such a smash hit?

AC   It's really well felt; it's believable, it's not phony. He's not just making it up because he thinks that would sound well. It seems to come straight from the heart, to use old-fashioned terms. The sense of continuity, the steadiness of the flow, the satisfaction of the arch that it creates from beginning to end are all very gratifying and make you believe the sincerity he obviously put into it.

PD   What about the professionals who say this feels like Puccini and we've heard it all before?

AC   I don't think that's fair. I don't see any Puccini in it. We've had it before in the sense that he wasn't breaking any new paths. He'd be closer to someone like Virgil Thomson than to our music, I suppose, though their temperaments are completely different. As far as musical idiom goes, Virgil was never a pathbreaker.

PD   You mention Thomson who, like you, had a connection with Paris. Is there a kind of European sophistication about Barber?

AC   I think there's something to that. It has the air of not being the music of a new country or of a man trying things out for the first time. It seems very well settled in its musical idiom—not experimental but very satisfying.

PD   It has been said, even by Barber himself, that he was a very lucky composer.

AC   It wouldn't have occurred to me to say that he was lucky. I'd say that he was well poised, he didn't seem to be reaching out for something he wasn't going to be able to accomplish.

PD   He was fortunate in managing to survive as a composer without having to take other work?

AC   We never thought of him as indigent or somebody really struggling to make a living. I don't know where the income came from exactly, but he always seemed well settled in a nice house doing what he wanted to do without having to hold down a job. That may not have been the actual truth, but that's the way it seemed.

PD   Do you think Barber and Menotti influenced each other?

AC   It's possible. I can't say I'm aware of Menotti's influence on Sam's music. Perhaps I'm more inclined to find Barber's influence on Menotti, although I'd hesitate to say that with any sense of security. They were both using a musical idiom that was sympathetic one to the other— rather old-fashioned and not at all trying to add a new page to the history of music. [*laughs*]

PD   Would you regard the dramatic intensity in some of Barber's works as related to his personal life?

AC   No. He certainly didn't give off an air of being inwardly turbulent. By comparison with other composers he seemed very set in his ways, well established, and well-to-do. I'd go so far as to say he was living a kind of bourgeois life, which [*laughs*] wasn't true of the rest of us for whom earning a living was much more precarious!

PD   And he got a publisher early on—Schirmer's—and stayed with them.

AC   That was lucky, of course. I wasn't so lucky because the big-shot publishers wouldn't touch me. I was a far-out modernist, the music was difficult to play, rhythms difficult to reproduce. I was thought to be a financial bust. We ended up finding a nice, rich American woman, very fond of music, who set us up into a publishing house.[6] She had a summer house

6. Alma Morgenthau Wertheim (1887–1953), divorced wife of New York banker Maurice Wertheim, was one of a number of influential women patrons of new music active in New York from the 1920s.

in Cos Cob, Connecticut, and we called it the Cos Cob Press. But Sam never had those problems. Schirmer's wouldn't touch the rest of us as being too far out!

AJ⁷   Did you ever visit Capricorn?

AC   Yes, I did visit Mt. Kisco. I was living not very far away, and it was easy to make the trip. I don't know what he thought of my music; I never asked him! [*laughs*] Probably in the early days he thought of me as a wild-eyed radical doing nutty things! But I'm not even sure of that. He was by nature very polite. He could say sharp, critical things, but the overall impression was of a man who didn't, as we say, shoot his mouth off. He thought about what he was going to say before he said it, considered it.

PD   Unlike you, Barber had music in the family. Did you ever hear any music by Sidney Homer, his uncle?

AC   I may have heard a song, but it made no lasting impression.

PD   Do you think Barber was particularly successful in smaller forms like songs?

AC   Well, you're making it sound too limiting. That may have been true, but I never thought of him as a songwriter but as a composer in the fullest sense, writing operas, fugues, and symphonies. He was one of our most accomplished composers, even in a technical sense . . .

PD   Is it this fine technique that ensures his survival?

AC   He wasn't carrying out what you would have thought a young composer would have wanted to do by writing things that other composers couldn't possibly have written. He wasn't ambitious to strike out on new paths, make a fuss, and upset audiences. I almost said "academic," but that would be wrong. He didn't try things that didn't come off, like some composers—perhaps it'll work, perhaps it won't.

PD   Are there conservative composers from other countries comparable to Barber?

AC   It wouldn't be comparable exactly, but I would think of Gabriel Fauré, living at a time just before Debussy and Ravel, writing in a very conservative idiom—by their standards—music that stands up beautifully in spite of the fact that it wasn't the latest thing.⁸

---

7. Arthur Johnson, BBC producer.
8. Gabriel Fauré (1845–1924). In 1923 Copland made an arrangement for string quartet of Fauré's ninth prelude for piano and wrote his Rondino based on the letters in Fauré's name. He followed this with one of his first published articles: "Gabriel Fauré, a Neglected Master," *Musical Quarterly* (October 1924): 573–86.

PD   Do you know enough of the music of Walton to make a comparison?[9]

AC   Not really, no. I think of Sam as more interested in expressing his personal feelings in his music and Walton as more of a big-shot type, giving you a sense of the grandiosities of our time and so forth. More extroverted. Sam was more moody; personally he could be quite moody, but I didn't know much of that.

PD   Is there anything you'd like to add to this portrait of Barber? I think we've covered everything.

AC   I think so too.

---

9. Sir William Walton (1902–83).

Chapter Nine

William Schuman

Interview with Peter Dickinson, 888 Park Avenue, New York City, May 14, 1981

Introduction

William Schuman (1910–92) made an influential contribution to American musical life as composer, teacher, and administrator. He was born in New York City and began serious study of music relatively late. He once explained: "It was not a matter of my being interested in baseball in my youth. It *was* my youth."[1] That essentially American sport gave him the subject of his only opera, *The Mighty Casey*, but he was energetically involved in various types of popular music and jazz at a time when his composer contemporaries were studying abroad. Schuman wrote songs with Edward B. Marks Jr. and Frank Loesser before they became household names, but the turning point came when he heard Toscanini conduct the New York Philharmonic in 1930. Schuman was nineteen and had reluctantly accompanied his sister to the concert. It changed his life and enabled him to recognize his future. He abruptly left his courses at the School of Commerce at New York University, but he never lost his business sense. The experience of seeing and hearing a large orchestra fueled his enthusiasm for the symphony in a way that carried through into his own substantial contributions to the form.

In the early 1930s Schuman gradually became a serious composer, but his melodic style was permanently affected by his work in popular song. Later he said that he wrote entirely by singing, not by sitting at the piano. His studies included summer courses at the Juilliard School of Music, of which he was later president, and—after he came across the Third Symphony—studies with Roy Harris. Schuman completed two degrees at Columbia University Teachers College and in 1935 took a teaching post at Sarah Lawrence College. Already, his

---

1. Cited in Christopher Rouse, *William Schuman: A Documentary* (New York: Theodore Presser/G. Schirmer, 1980), 1. See also Joseph W. Polisi, *American Muse: The Life and Times of William Schuman* (London: Amadeus, 2009).

separate strands of composer, educator, and visionary planner began to interact. He was able to try out his theories on the students, especially the notion of teaching music from actual music rather than using mere academic models.

In 1938 Schuman's Second Symphony attracted the attention of Koussevitzky, who conducted it with the Boston Symphony, although Schuman later withdrew the work. In 1941 his Third Symphony won the first New York Music Critics Circle Award, and the following year his choral work *A Free Song* earned the first of his two Pulitzer Prizes. In 1943 his Fifth Symphony, for strings, was acclaimed; these successes quickly established Schuman's reputation.

In 1938 Copland wrote, "Schuman is . . . the musical find of the year . . . a composer who is going places."[2] Thirty-three years later he added: "In Schuman's pieces you have the feeling that only an American could have written them. . . . [Y]ou hear it in the kind of American optimism which is the base of his music."[3]

Even so, Schuman could not satisfy his creative drive solely through composition. When the Juilliard School of Music needed a new president in 1945, he took over a conservative institution that would soon be known for the Juilliard Quartet, the formation of a Dance Division, and the innovative Literature and Materials of Music program.

Schuman became the founding president of Lincoln Center in 1962, and his composing continued to go hand in hand with his duties as a public figure. His Eighth Symphony was commissioned for the opening of Philharmonic Hall, and Schuman launched Alice Tully Hall in 1969. Leonard Bernstein paid tribute: "Through his unique combination of intellect and spirit, he has lent an originality and grandeur of concept to the whole project that it could easily have lacked without him."[4] Schuman was a natural statesman, lavishly honored, and a lifelong supporter of American composers and performers.

Interview

By Permission of Anthony Schuman

WS   If you ask me how Samuel Barber managed to be such a wonderful composer, leaving such a wonderful literature, and also left his heirs $1 million, my reply might sound bitter—I'm a family man and he wasn't. I assure you if he'd been a family man, there would have been no million

---

2. Oliver Daniel, *William Schuman*, BMI catalog, 1973, 1 (quoted from *Modern Music*, May 1938).

3. Remarks made when Copland presented the medal of the MacDowell Colony to Schuman in 1971. Quoted in ibid, 3.

4. Quoted in Rouse, *William Schuman: A Documentary*, 23.

dollars: he might have left some offspring with college degrees, and that would have taken care of the excess cash!

On the other hand, to give you a more serious answer, Sam was very widely performed and deservedly so, and he also had the good luck—in addition to his large works, which weren't so often performed—to have written several smaller pieces that were capable of easy performance. That doesn't mean they were any less excellent because they weren't, but, obviously, the *Adagio for Strings* is in anybody's all-time hit parade. If you have five hundred performances of that every year for twenty-five years, you have a very high rating in the performing rights society. Also, I do not know what he inherited from his family. I know nothing about that personal side of his life. I never inquired because we didn't have that kind of relationship, although I have to tell you that I hadn't seen Sam for several years and we met outside Alice Tully Hall where the Chamber Music Society, of which I'm an officer, had commissioned him to do some songs.[5] He said: "Bill, listen, you're going to be sixty-five. For heaven's sake, don't forget to put in for your Medicare." These were two composers meeting after not having seen each other for some time!

I had that kind of marvelous bantering relationship to Sam, although sometimes we exchanged letters. On my study wall over there is a picture of the two of us taken at the time of *Antony and Cleopatra*. I was president of the Lincoln Center then, and I said to Rudolf Bing: "You have to commission a new work for the opening of the new house at Lincoln Center, and it's got to be an American composer. I'm not the one you're talking about because I'm not an opera writer. There are several you might commission, but you've got to do that." Some months later, when I was called upon to make some remarks about Bing, I said: "Rudolph Bing chose Samuel Barber for two reasons. The first is that he genuinely admires Barber's music, and the second is that he doesn't know the name of any other American composer!"[6] [*laughs*] And Sam absolutely loved that story—he was present—and he had that kind of appreciative wit even when he was the butt of the joke.

But I wouldn't leave you with the feeling that it was all just bantering. When we met we did indeed discuss serious things, and I was very touched when Gian Carlo Menotti called me and asked whether my wife

5. *Three Songs*, op. 72 (1972), premiered by Dietrich Fischer-Dieskau at Alice Tully Hall, April 30, 1974.

6. Rudolf Bing (1902–97), Austrian-born British impresario who was general manager of Glyndebourne Opera (1936–49) and the Met (1950–72). He was a formidable figure who raised the standards of opera performance.

and I would come to the hospital just about a week before Sam died. That was an extraordinary time. I asked Gian Carlo whether I should speak to Sam, because I had just been in Pittsburgh and heard the performance André Previn gave of his *Third Essay*.[7] I told André, "This is not Sam's latest composition—it's his last composition." [At the hospital] we started talking about it and Gian Carlo said, "Sam, Bill's here and wants to tell you about it." And I got through to him, which was quite remarkable. He recognized me on that extraordinary afternoon and I shall never, never forget it.

PD   What is it that creates the impact of the *Adagio for Strings?*

WS   The reason the *Adagio* makes the effect it does is because it's a perfect piece of music—like Mendelssohn's Violin Concerto. It wasn't the deepest piece that Sam ever wrote, but it was an early piece and has within it, I would say, all the gestures, rhetoric, and characteristics that would be later so fully and gloriously developed by him. I think it works because it's so precise emotionally. The emotional climate is never left in doubt. It begins, reaches its climax, makes its point, and goes away. Every time you hear a first-class performance it's quite an experience. For me it's never a warhorse. I'm always moved by it.

PD   We've had various reactions ranging from death to a love scene.

WS   I think whether it's a love scene or a death scene depends upon one's attitude to love and life. I could not possibly characterize it so specifically. To me it's merely a good piece. The other day a young composer, knowing I was doing a new piece for the St. Louis Orchestra and its centenary, asked me, "What statement are you trying to make?" I said: "What statement? How old are you? I'm trying to write a good piece—that's all."[8] I think that's what Sam was trying to do—it's what every composer tries to do. That's not so easy.

PD   Are there any technical things in the *Adagio* that you can identify?

WS   I find that I would be hard-pressed to say technically why the work is such a success. I think one reason is that you're not aware of any technique at all. It all seems quite effortless, quite natural. I think that's what happens with a good piece of music. But on the other hand, I also think that about his more complicated works. I was driving the car and had

---

7. *Third Essay for Orchestra*, op. 47 (1978). See interview with Barber conducted by Robert Sherman, chapter 4. André Previn (1929–), German-born American conductor, pianist, and composer.

8. *American Hymn: Orchestral Variations on a Original Theme*, premiered by the St. Louis Symphony Orchestra on September 24, 1982, under Leonard Slatkin.

the radio on and was listening to a cello concerto, and it took me quite a while before I realized it was Sam's. This is a thing I always feel about his music—it's perfectly made. That's not a put-down. To me that's very high praise indeed, although there are perhaps great works in the world that you could say weren't perfect. Everybody likes to talk about the third movement of the *Eroica* not being perfect. We should have more such imperfect pieces! [*laughs*]

PD   You heard the Barber Cello Concerto on the radio without recognizing it as Barber. Does that matter? If it had been Copland you'd have known right away.

WS   You know a piece of Aaron's because of the well-known Copland sound. Other people may not have a sound that is their own, but they have an orchestral style that is immediately recognizable. I can think of all sorts of composers, living and of the past, where you hear it and immediately know whose piece it is. You could tune in on a piece of Barber and if you didn't know it that well—I'd forgotten a lot of the Cello Concerto—it might take a little while. I didn't think it was Prokofiev, mind you, but sections of it could have been the international-type musical language of the twentieth century, whereas other composers have quite a precise language. I don't think that's a qualitative judgment I'm making; I'm try-ing to say something descriptive. I remember going into a concert hall with Aaron and hearing a new piece of Elliott Carter's. Aaron said, "If you didn't know that was Elliott's piece, could you say what composer it was?" I said, "No." And that's in no way to take away from his extraordi-nary achievements. It's just that different composers have different kinds of identities, and some are more precise than others. As you gather, I like to listen to music while I drive—you have to do something—and I often hear pieces out of the nineteenth-century literature that I know are not by Brahms because you know all the Brahms pieces. But then it turns out to be somebody else, a watered-down version that might be a piece of Dvořák that you didn't know—or Delius. If you didn't know the pieces, you might confuse it with some other impressionistic composer. The reason I keep emphasizing that these are not qualitative judgments is that music is filled with all sorts of glorious variations on the techniques composers use and the degree of precise identification each composer has. To give this a qualitative importance is just as foolish as saying that nationalism is important. It isn't.

PD   We may have gone overboard in hunting for individuality. After the *Ada-gio,* what are some other high points?

WS   One night there was a broadcast of *Vanessa,* and I was so moved by it that I wrote to Sam and said that those final pages are among the most beautiful in the entire literature of operatic music. When I wrote to him he sent me a marvelous letter thanking me for what I said: "I may as well tell you that secretly I've always been very jealous of the big crescendo in your Third Symphony!" [*laughs*]

Thinking of other mature works of Sam's, I was at the first performance of the *Hermit Songs* given by Leontyne Price at the home of her teacher Florence Page Kimball with Barber at the piano.[9] That was one of the great experiences I recall of hearing new music. Those songs have held up very well. I simply respond positively to Barber's music. It doesn't mean I respond to every piece he's written—I don't respond to every piece I've written myself! I've withdrawn a number; perhaps I should have withdrawn more. The point is that among his great works he's left a very important legacy.

PD   He's a very different composer from you.

WS   Oh, yes, and we were always talked about together because we were born in the same year but obviously are very different composers. A few years ago Sam won the Gold Medal for Music at the American Academy and Institute of Arts and Letters. That's a highly prestigious award; I was delighted he won it, and I was one who supported his nomination and was asked therefore to make the presentation. We were having lunch before and Sam said, "Now, what are you going to say?" I said, "Look, this is a formal occasion and I'm prepared. The important thing, Sam, is what are you going to say?" I love to speak in public; it's always a joy for me. Sam didn't like it at all; he rarely did it. He said, "Do I have to say something?" I said, "You absolutely do." This is what I said:

There is an ancient saying that two vinegar salesmen cannot be friends. In these surroundings we have nothing but exceptions to this thesis. We glory in giving awards to the young and later on medals to each other. Samuel Barber and I have been friends and colleagues since the 1930s. We were both born in the same year, but since I am five months his junior it is a special joy for me today to pay my respects to an older colleague and honor him for his extraordinary achievements. The history of the arts is filled with examples of those who expanded the means of expression. There have, however, been other artists who are content to create within established means. In music such composers would include Bach, Mozart, Mendelssohn, and Brahms. Samuel Barber is in this tradition. Barber's work is widely recognized and accepted as having enriched the literature of virtually every facet of musical expression. Each piece

---

9. *Hermit Songs*, op. 29 (1953).

that he has created is characterized by deeply felt emotions couched in the sophisticated terms of a master craftsman. If one were to choose a single word best to describe his art, the choice would have to be "impeccable." Now at the height of his powers we salute Samuel Barber and present him with this symbol of the high esteem and affection in which he is held by his appreciative colleagues.

Sam said, by way of reply, "I have no prepared speech, but what I say will be even more brief than Mr. Schuman's. I remember the shortest speech I ever heard was at W. H. Auden's in that rather rundown house in St. Mark's Place at one of his birthday parties, which I shall never forget. Edith Sitwell was there, and he asked me if I would go over and speak to her.[10] He said: 'Don't call her Dame Edith but call her Dr. Edith because she has just received a doctorate from Oxford and she prefers to be called Dr.' So I went over and she was sitting on a broken-down armchair about three inches from the ground. It was impossible to talk in that position and I leaned over and said: 'Dr. Edith, it's really awfully difficult to talk to you in this position' and she said: 'Don't—thank you.'" Then he sat down. [*laughs*][11]

That, to me, summarizes Sam's wit. In the summer of 1980 he won another award, which has become equal in distinction to the American Academy—that's the MacDowell Colony Award for contribution to the arts. Since I am chairman of the colony I was to have the privilege of presenting it to him, but he wasn't really quite well enough to come. He called me and said he was going to Paris the next day to hear a production of *Vanessa* and would leave immediately so as not to read the reviews. That's when he went to Gian Carlo's house in Scotland. I told this story at the colony: we missed him, but in his absence we played the *Summer Music*—it was wonderful to hear it up there in those beautiful hills.

Sam was one of the few contemporary composers who lived completely as a composer. I'm not talking economics because a number of us can make out economically now, but he lived a composer's life because that's all he did. He was a great scholar, prodigious reader, highly cultivated, brilliant linguist—he was all these things, but he was not given to social causes. He was not a man who joined with the rest of us in our composers' alliances and in working for federal support of the arts. That was not his nature: he was a loner. He was very witty, very private, and he had his inner circle

10. Dame Edith Sitwell (1887–1964), leading British poet, sister of Osbert and Sacheverell.

11. Proceedings of the American Academy and Institute of Arts and Letters, 2nd series, no. 27 (New York: American Academy and Institute of Arts and Letters, 1977).

of friends. He lived just a few blocks from here at 72nd and Fifth. Two or three years ago at one of his in-between birthdays it was very surprising that he threw a great big party, had all the furniture taken out of the apartment, and had tables set up as though it was some banquet. John Browning played there; Sam sat on a little dais; different people spoke. It was absolutely atypical—I don't know what got into him to do that, but he did.

PD   Was his music influenced by Menotti?

WS   No. I think Barber is a very different musical personality than Menotti. He was primarily a theater composer, so the music per se carries out the wishes of the dramatist, whereas Sam was primarily a composer. Of course, they had a very close relationship. I have never seen the slightest influence on Barber's music of Menotti. If it's there it escapes me.

PD   Perhaps the other way round?

WS   I wouldn't think Barber influenced Menotti musically either, from having heard Menotti's music.

PD   So, finally, the summit of his achievement in music of all kinds?

WS   There are so many individual examples one could cite but, looking at them in their entirety, perhaps the most typical and most glorious example of Barber at the height of his powers would be those final pages of *Vanessa.*

Chapter Ten

Virgil Thomson

Interview with Peter Dickinson, Chelsea Hotel, New York City, May 12, 1981

Introduction

Virgil Thomson (1896–1989) was born in Kansas City, Missouri, and died in New York City. His upbringing was centered on the Baptist Church and its musical heritage. He was an organist and, after army training, entered Harvard in 1919. There he began a lifetime's devotion to French music, accompanied the Harvard Glee Club, encountered the music of Erik Satie and the writings of Gertrude Stein—he said they changed his life[1]—and began to compose. He spent a year in Paris studying with Nadia Boulanger; then, back at Harvard in 1923, he gave the American premiere of Satie's *Socrate*. In 1925 he returned to Paris, where he lived until 1940. He met Gertrude Stein in 1926 and immediately started setting her words to music. Their two operas, *Four Saints in Three Acts* and *Mother of Us All*, were pioneering examples of the non-narrative musical theater developed later by Philip Glass and others.[2] Thomson said, "[I]t was by the discipline of spontaneity, which I had come into contact with through reading Gertrude Stein, that made my music simple."[3] I took this parallel further, with the composer's approval: "Thomson comes closer than any other composer to reflecting the literary techniques of Stein in music by means of

---

1. Thomson, *Virgil Thomson* (New York: A. A. Knopf, 1966), 46.
2. Philip Glass (1937–), the most successful minimalist composer, who studied both at Juilliard and in Paris with Nadia Boulanger and Ravi Shankar. He founded his own ensemble, which toured internationally. Glass has become widely known through his operas and film collaborations.
3. John Rockwell, "A Conversation with Virgil Thomson," *Poetry in Review* (Spring-Summer 1977): 419. Also in Thomson, *A Virgil Thomson Reader* (Boston: Houghton Mifflin, 1981), 427–41.

the same short-circuiting from poetry to music which she herself had experienced earlier from painting to writing."[4]

During his years in Paris, Thomson began writing documentary film scores, anticipating Copland in this medium, and perfected his own type of musical portraits composed in front of the sitter. On returning to New York he became highly influential as chief music critic of *The Herald Tribune* from 1940 to 1954. In an obituary tribute I wrote: "Virgil Thomson was a composer and writer of originality, courage and wit formed by a unique mixture of American and French influences. . . . He came from a generation of American composers which had to find its own way without benefit of university patronage. In that kind of free market he thrived and survived—and so will the best of his music."[5]

Thomson periodically commented on Barber's music. In 1943 he wrote, "Private Samuel Barber's *Essay for Orchestra No. 1* is a pretty piece but not a very strong one."[6] In the 1940s and 1950s he unreservedly admired the Cello Concerto and *Medea*. In reviewing Wilfrid Mellers's *Music in a New Found Land* he queried: "Whether Samuel Barber's music is mainly an evocation of adolescence, like Tchaikovsky's and Rachmaninoff's, anyone can argue." And he gave a 1960s verdict on Barber's music: "Certainly, for all its sweetness and fine workmanship, it is no part just now of our intellectual life."[7]

According to Thomson, Barber noted the success of his opera *Mother of Us All* in 1946. Unsurprisingly, he must have found it naïve since he said to Thomson, "I hope you won't mind my stealing a few of your chords!"[8]

Interview

By Permission of the Virgil Thomson Foundation Ltd.

We clarified that the BBC program was for radio, not TV, and then Thomson said that Charles "Chuck" Turner knew more about Barber than anyone else did.[9]

---

4. Dickinson, "Stein Satie Cummings Thomson Berners Cage: Toward a Context for the Music of Virgil Thomson," *Musical Quarterly* 72, 3 (1986): 394–409. This article began as a paper delivered in the composer's presence at the 1982 Special Joint Meeting of the Sonneck Society (now the Society for American Music) and other organizations in Lawrence, Kansas, on April 1, 1982. On March 2, 1988, after reading the article, Thomson wrote to me: "I remember the speech at Lawrence, Kansas, and am still wildly impressed by it."

5. Dickinson, "Obituary: Virgil Thomson," *Independent* (London), October 2, 1989.

6. Anthony Tommasini, *Virgil Thomson: Composer on the Aisle* (New York: Norton, 1997), 362.

7. Quoted in "On Being Discussed," *New York Review of Books*, June 3, 1965.

8. Thomson, *Virgil Thomson*, 384.

9. See interview with Charles Turner, chapter 7.

VT [His career was not particularly] interesting or eventful. It consisted
of first performances and glorious occasions, standing ovations, and
large checks because he made more money than anybody. His take at
ASCAP—I don't know what it is, but it's very high. He had successful
works played all over the world all the time. The Piano Concerto he
wrote for John Browning had had over two hundred performances ten
years ago—it's been everywhere.

Sam's music travels well; it repeats well because it's extremely well constructed. It's not vulgar in its material or in its appeal. It's very high-class
but not hard to take. He was a good businessman, getting $50,000 for com-
missions. I think Chuck told me he'd been offered a commission, which he
couldn't take because he wasn't well, for $100,000. That's real money!

PD Which pieces are most likely to survive?

VT How would I know?

PD I was told about the launch party for *Grove's Dictionary* when you said
you were going to enjoy the second volume with Bach, Beethoven—and
Barber![10]

VT Oh, I [ought to have] mentioned Britten out of courtesy [*laughs*] and
Bernstein, who was there.

PD But you did say Barber, and I'd be interested to know which you think
are the high points.

VT I wouldn't know.

PD But you were working as a critic in New York as Barber's works came out.

VT I don't rank people or mark them like examinations. The piece that I'm
sure had the largest number of performances is the famous *Adagio for
Strings*. I know the piece well because I've conducted it. I can understand
its popularity because it's music that lets itself be conducted; it's a pleasure to interpret it. Just like Meriel knows that there are certain vocal
pieces that are rewarding.[11] People don't get tired of it. It's not silly.

PD We tend to look for composers' personalities in their music—it's easy to
recognize yours—but how does Barber's personality come out?

---

10. Stanley Sadie, ed., *The New Grove Dictionary of Music and Musicians* (London: Macmillan, 1980).

11. Meriel Dickinson (1940–), British mezzo-soprano, who made first recordings of
Thomson's *Portrait of FB* and *Two by Marianne Moore* on Unicorn LP RHS 353 (1978).
Thomson listened to the test pressing in London and after an anxious pause proclaimed
"that's everything it oughta be!"

VT   Well, I don't know. It isn't so much the personality but the whole buildup
     of character and history. He was brought up in a well-to-do family; he's
     never lacked for money; they were people of some distinction, and his aunt
     was a very famous opera singer. Her husband was a composer of not undis-
     tinguished songs. Sam had perfectly good vocal lessons as a young man
     and could sing, would probably have had a career as a singer if his voice
     had been stronger. He could always sing elegantly and clearly—there is a
     record.[12] He went to the Curtis Institute where his teacher of, I presume,
     counterpoint and composition was Rosario Scalero. I knew him well because
     I had lessons from him too, but not at Curtis. He was a tall and distinguished
     Italian who had lived in Vienna for some years and had been a pupil of a
     close friend of Brahms. Scalero taught counterpoint straight out of Fux.[13]
     I had already been through the Paris strict counterpoint with Nadia Bou-
     langer, but he said I'd have to do it again.[14] It was hard to find out what the
     differences were between his teaching and hers except that he was a little
     more tolerant of 6/4 chords than she was! [*laughs*] He would have noth-
     ing to do with a special kind of exercise we had in Paris called *mélange a
     quatre parties*—four species all together. He was something of a disappointed
     composer but a very well-trained musician, and he gave both Sam and Gian
     Carlo Menotti good discipline in harmony and counterpoint. Along with this
     he continually insisted that there was a kind of norm. He was separate from
     the French idea of experiment, and he had never been bitten by the little
     animal that makes you itch to be modern. His idea was that you wrote cho-
     rales like Bach and sonatas and overtures like Brahms. Now that training for
     Sam and Gian Carlo during their formative years kept them away from the
     infection of the modernist ideal and hopes. Also way off in Philadelphia . . .

PD   Did it also keep them away from being American?

VT   Sam was not interested in Americana. Gian Carlo could have put some-
     thing like that into an opera and, I think, once or twice did. In the same
     way that Benjy Britten put in a bit of jazz—or early–nineteenth-century
     dance hall by the seashore! [*laughs*] It was a dramatic idea, one that any-
     body could understand, and he imitated it perfectly well.

---

12. Barber recorded *Dover Beach* with the Curtis String Quartet on May 13, 1935, on
CD Pearl GEM0049.

13. Johann Joseph Fux (1660–1741), Austrian composer and theorist whose *Gradus ad
Parnassum* (1725) was an influential study of contrapuntal techniques.

14. Thomson was in New York for the 1923–24 season and took lessons with Scalero:
"[H]aving no faith in French music-teaching, he was putting me through strict counter-
point again. . . . I never showed him any of my pieces." Thomson, *Virgil Thomson*, 68–69.
Nadia Boulanger (1887–1979), influential French composition teacher whose many
American pupils included Carter and Copland.

PD Does it matter if a composer doesn't come to terms with popular culture? Stravinsky was involved with folk music and African American idioms.

VT The Russians always had to do with folk music. The folk element is much closer to the Russian intellectual mind than it is in Germany, where it's pretty far away, and in Italy it's another level. There are plenty of American composers who never did anything about folklore. I don't think MacDowell did, to speak of, or Ives's teacher Horatio Parker.[15] He was an organist who wrote oratorios in the British manner, which are still given in England, the home of the oratorio.

PD I know you admire MacDowell, and you've even been controversial in saying he might survive longer than Ives! [*laughs*]

VT It was just a crack.

PD What about comparing Barber with MacDowell? Would that be fair?

VT No. Everything was different—the education, the social class, and the musical instruction. Barber had European musical instruction in Philadelphia, which is almost *huis clos,*[16] whereas MacDowell studied in Germany and a bit in Paris in the time when the Grieg and Dvořák models were available in Europe for imitation—a kind of nationalism as a field of operation. They were different kinds of people. I never knew MacDowell. The people who attended his classes at Columbia thought he was quite wonderful as a teacher—sort of music appreciation he did, before that became a racket.[17] Sam was closed in on himself. The other element in his preparation, which was very characteristic beside the Italian-Brahms education, was that he got a Prix de Rome quite early and went to live in Italy. He was subjected to the very reactionary musical life of Italy, whereas the rest of us had all been to Paris. And before Paris, possibly Harvard and places like that, which were outposts.

PD Do you feel that knowing Menotti affected Barber's move toward opera or even the kind of music he wrote?

VT Well, I can't give you the entire communication on the subject of opera because I wasn't present when they were writing operas together. It was clear from the beginning that Sam did not have very much the *sens du theatre.* He didn't feel at home on the stage. He was a chamber music and

---

15. Edward MacDowell (1860–1908) drew on American Indian music. Horatio Parker (1863–1919), pupil of Josef Rheinberger (1839–1901).

16. Implying isolation.

17. For Thomson's vicious demolition of the "music appreciation racket," see *The State of Music* (New York: Vintage Books, 1962), 111–20.

song composer. Left to himself, he would probably not have taken up opera or, if he did, would have done what so many of the song composers do, which is to substitute for a dramatic progress a kind of Stations of the Cross, like a song cycle. Here's a moment and you write a piece about it, then here's another moment. . . . Haydn was like that. He wrote over two dozen operas, but every number holds up the show. The Handel operas move forward and Mozart's perfectly, but Beethoven made pieces without too much dramatic compulsion or trajectory. When the Metropolitan and various other commissioning sources kept thinking they would get operas out of Sam, Gian Carlo could very well have said, "Oh come on, try it, Sam. I'll write you a libretto." The first one was *Vanessa*, then there was *Antony and Cleopatra* with the Italian director Zeffirelli.[18] He was a public danger! [*laughs*] He's flopped more shows . . .

PD   Menotti told us that he arranged *Vanessa* so it contained special things that would appeal to Barber . . .

VT   Those are the numbers.

PD   . . . and the character music and the dances. Then when it came to *Antony and Cleopatra* he hadn't done the libretto but helped with the revision.

VT   That's where he came in. Sam was not by nature a theater composer. He did pretty well with ballets, particularly for Martha Graham.[19] The operas are not proper operas and he never tried films. He was an introspective composer—concertos, symphonic pieces, string quartets, plus a great deal of vocal music.

PD   Is it as a song composer that he's been given the highest acclaim?

VT   I don't know about that because I don't follow those things. I don't grade people myself, and I don't take too seriously other people's grading because it usually turns out to be what sells best or what gets the best reviews.

PD   I don't mean that I agree with that approach, but could you compare him with composers of other countries?

---

18. See Ned Rorem, "Franco Zeffirelli," in *A Ned Rorem Reader* (New Haven: Yale University Press, 2001), 246–51.

19. Martha Graham (1894–1991), pioneering modern dance choreographer who used Copland's music for *Appalachian Spring* (1944). She used Barber's *Medea*, op. 23 (1946) for her ballet *Serpent Heart* (1946), followed by various titles and revisions; then *Frescoes* (1978), two scenes from *Antony and Cleopatra*, op. 40, taken from the opera in 1968; and *Andromache's Lament* (1982) using *Andromache's Farewell*, Op 39, 1962.

VT   I don't know of an opposite number. I know some other examples—Britten and Shostakovich are definitely a pair. Very similar in their approach and the nature of their success. I don't know of anybody quite like Sam Barber in Europe. In France they're all on the modern side. In Italy they all write operas—and sort of pull them off.

PD   I wonder whether there's something in common with Walton[20]—a lyrical line, operas . . .

VT   Yes, yes. That would work.

PD   Or Lennox Berkeley?[21]

VT   Sam is more successful. When his music comes off, it does so quite beautifully. Even in the operas there are nuggets. I don't know the choral work *Prayers of Kierkegaard,* but conductors tell me it's quite wonderful.[22] *Knoxville: Summer of 1915* has been vastly successful, and it goes on.[23]

PD   Is that the song composer's approach to the voice?

VT   A gentle text, made out of a prose poem by James Agee. It's all about a region that's not too different from southern Pennsylvania where he was brought up—I mean sociologically. I think Sam felt at home with the Agee text.

PD   It's got the colloquial treatment of the English language that must appeal to you?

VT   It never occurred to me to put it to music, but if it had I could have done it.

      I conducted Sam's early overture *School for Scandal* and the *Adagio for Strings,* which, as you know, is out of the string quartet, but it works better in the full string version.

PD   There's a version for voices too. I wonder whether Barber minded being overwhelmingly known as the composer of the *Adagio for Strings?*

---

20. Sir William Walton (1902–83). Thomson is more ready to accept this comparison than Copland is—see the latter's interview in chapter 8.

21. Sir Lennox Berkeley (1903–89).

22. *Prayers of Kierkegaard,* op. 30, soprano and orchestra (1954), premiered by Leontyne Price on December 3, 1954, with Jean Kraft (contralto), Edward Munro (tenor), the Cecilia Society Chorus, director Hugh Ross, and the Boston Symphony Orchestra under Charles Munch, at Symphony Hall, Boston.

23. *Knoxville: Summer of 1915,* op. 24, for soprano and orchestra (1948), text by James Agee, premiere by Eleanor Steber on April 9, 1948, with the Boston Symphony under Serge Koussevizsky.

VT   You never mind something that's successful. Does it have words, this choral version?

PD   Yes, the *Agnus Dei.*

VT   Since I know the *Adagio* quite well from the inside, I would propose a guess at the subject matter. I think it's a love scene, a detailed love scene—bed scene. I suspect that is probably the reason why conductors like to conduct it and why audiences like to listen to it because they can feel that without openly identifying—maybe they do or do not identify in their minds. I think that's what it is. So you make an *Agnus Dei* out of it![24] [*laughs*] It'll work. But it's an awful lot of rubbing around! [*laughs*]

PD   That's fascinating because the piece has got this shape, reaching a climax with high pitch and then decay?

VT   Oh, yes!

PD   You think that accounts for its universal appeal?

VT   I think it's a very smooth [*laughs*] successful love scene. Not a dramatic one but a very satisfactory one. [*laughs*] As I say, with constant rubbings among the voices there. I never asked Sam. Why should I? I don't like to tell people what their music is about.

PD   Successful salon pieces by the romantic composers often had that shape, with a climax three-quarters of the way through.

VT   Well, Sam was a romantic composer, of course. The instrumental pieces may tend toward similar shapes, but the works with vocal texts do not all come out alike.

PD   Some of the vocal pieces are very anguished: *Andromache's Farewell,* where she won't see her son again because he's going to be murdered, and *The Lovers,* about devastatingly unhappy love.[25]

VT   Anybody can imagine himself as unhappy in love and getting inspired by it. Everybody works more or less the same way. You think you're putting yourself into your pieces, or you think you're leaving yourself out. Of course, you're always there in one form or another.

---

24. Arranged for chorus (1967). Thomson would have been interested to know that "visitors were particularly amused by Sam Taylor-Wood's video of a naked man dancing to the *Adagio*" shown at the Tate Modern, London, in 2008. "The Definitive Guide to Modern British Art," *The Times,* October 25, 2008.

25. *Andromache's Farewell* (Euripides), op. 39, soprano and orchestra (1962); *The Lovers* (Pablo Neruda), op. 43, baritone and orchestra (1971).

Sam wrote easily, I think, but very carefully and not too fast. I remember [*laughs*] Heinsheimer at Schirmer's saying to me: "The trouble with you is you write too much music. Now, Sam writes just the right amount for a publisher. Every year there's one major work and one or two little ones. That I can merchandise."

PD   Do you remember any typical incidents that show Barber's character?

VT   I think you'll get those better out of Chuck Turner, who remembers all sorts of things and saw Sam Barber more often than I ever did. Sam could be very charming when he set out to be because he was awfully good-looking. If he wished to turn on the manners and the charm, it could work very nicely. But very easily he would get angry and turn mean. Oh, Sam could be quite awful and say cruel things to people.

AJ   You said he was a very urbane man.

VT   I didn't use the term. I'm not sure what urbane would mean in my language. He was *bien elevé* in the French sense. He came from a good family, knew how to hold his forks and spoons. [*laughs*] In that way Sam was rather like some of our English friends, brought up to good manners and if left alone and not annoyed they will use them. But if annoyed they will attack.

PD   We've heard that he served in ASCAP and such organizations.

VT   Sam did not like serving on committees, but at one point he realized that ASCAP was not paying the serious composers the amount of money he thought they could. He spoke to two or three people there, and several composers got together and pressed them to make a better arrangement—which they did. Then he never did anything more. To satisfy me—although he never really cared whether he pleased anybody or not—he did serve as one of the plaintiffs in a lawsuit known as the ASCAP suit against the broadcasters for moving in combination in restraint of trade monopoly. There was a whole batch of plaintiffs of whom Sam was one, and he contributed some money to that—he rather regretted it when we didn't win the suit. I was on the committee, which met regularly. I'm much more of a committee member than Sam was. Gian Carlo would be a committee member if he were ever in the same place long enough because he's sort of a solid citizen. Actually, Gian Carlo's testimony in the pre-trial examinations that went on for several years was quite brilliant. What else do you want know?

PD   I never got a mention from you of any pieces apart from the *Adagio.*

VT   I don't know works unless I've performed or conducted them. I became quite well acquainted through print with one of the essays for orchestra through being asked to review it for *Notes,* the magazine published by the Library of Congress. I examined it very carefully, wrote the review, and ventured an opinion of what the subject matter was. I think it was something about World War II. He had something of a success with another World War II piece about a stopwatch.[26]

PD The setting of Stephen Spender, *A Stopwatch and an Ordinance Map.*

VT Sam had many close associates among the novelists and particularly among the poets. Many of them he set to music. Chuck pointed out to me not long ago that as Sam got older he seemed to have less confidence in his own intellectual powers and sort of dropped those people or didn't make new friends in that domain. Sam didn't have any fancy education except the musical one. He didn't go to a university and get that familiarity with the intellectual machinery that people do have if they've been around Harvard, Oxford, or places like that.

PD Barber's early pieces remind me of some of Britten's initial successes.

VT Sam was a natural, a facile composer, as Britten was. They both have a large choral repertory, less purely orchestral. Britten had a stage sense. He could even put a lousy libretto on the stage sometimes, and when he had a good libretto he made fine stage pieces. Sam did not have a stage sense. Neither did Bach, Beethoven, or Brahms. Mozart, Bizet, Verdi, and Wagner all did. Wagner was formidable with these long acts in which people stand in the same place for half an hour singing the same music! They're still on the stage.

PD It's interesting that Barber opens the *Adagio* with an old-fashioned traditional 4/3 suspension. Nobody else at that time would have dared to do that.

VT Everything he did was of the old-fashioned type. The question of fashion didn't impress him in the least. His earliest experiences as a composer— under age twenty—were successful, and he had the sense to stay with what he'd been educated to do and what he could do well. He was very much upset by the failure of *Antony and Cleopatra* and went into retirement for two or three years and wouldn't see anybody. He didn't want to be questioned about it or have it mentioned. According to Chuck, he didn't write much music at that time. He really had a blow. But being formed in Italy to understand the Italians and their language, he trusted

26. *A Stopwatch and an Ordinance Map* (Stephen Spender), op. 15, for male chorus and timpani (1940), premiered at the Curtis Institute by the Curtis Institute Madrigal Chorus with David Stephens (timpani), under Barber, April 13, 1940.

this guy [Zeffirelli]. I don't know whether Gian Carlo, who had such good theater sense, was away or just letting the situation alone. There's every reason why the work should not have been successful. I don't think any opera on a Shakespeare text has ever been successful except in a foreign language. With one exception—Britten's *Midsummer Night's Dream*.[27] The *Macbeths*, the *Hamlets*, and the *Lears*—they're all in French, German, or Italian. You get rid of the Shakespeare! He won't take music! Sam might have been wary of that, but he wasn't. He didn't understand the nature of dramatic composition. Also—and this has flopped many a theater production of that play—there is not a love scene in it. I know that show backward; I've done music for it.[28] They talk about love, but what can you do with an opera without a love scene? It's a political play straight out of Plutarch all about how a great commander was betrayed by his girlfriend who ran away at the big battle. I think the lack of a love scene must have been deliberate on Shakespeare's part because the two main characters, Antony and Cleopatra, are both middle-aged. He was in his fifties and she was in her late thirties when they met. By the time the play is over she'd had two children—they were a kind of family. *Romeo and Juliet* is OK because the boys from the Choir School could play very young lovers and you could think they were girls. But boys are not going to play middle-aged ladies—at least if they do, middle-aged love on the stage might get a terrible laugh in London! [*laughs*]

PD   Which brings us back to the *Adagio for Strings*, which, according to you, does have the love scene.

VT   [*laughs*] There's nothing in either of those operas that is as continuous in an emotional pattern as the *Adagio*.

PD   Which doesn't work so well in the String Quartet?

VT   I think I've never heard the String Quartet. I've heard the Cello Concerto, the Piano Concerto—both very successful concertos. And the violin one. Sam was not a string player, but he could learn things. And he had a good ear. And it somehow runs through that upper–middle-class family and the very high-class artistic situation of Louise Homer. He was brought up to believe in the highest standards of artistic integrity. He never wrote down to anybody. He'd have one piece a little better than another, although I must say the workmanship, being extremely careful, holds up in an extraordinary way.

---

27. Benjamin Britten (1913–76); *A Midsummer Night's Dream* (1960).

28. Thomson wrote music for a production of *Antony and Cleopatra* starring Tallulah Bankhead. It opened in Rochester on October 13, 1937, and played in other cities, but it was not a success.

PD   Some people have suggested that he wrote music that he knew would be popular.

VT   I think that his idea of a successful musical work—I mean artistically successful—was something that could be played not necessarily in the pop concerts but for the subscription public of the Philadelphia Orchestra. Now, that's high middle-brow. If that's his ideal, it's not far from that of Rachmaninoff, who also lived in Philadelphia. It's not far from Britten but arrived at differently. His relation to the British success establishment, the immortality machine, is different from anything that takes place here because we have no such thing. They have it in France and Germany—God knows they have it in Russia! But I think the British one is the strongest in the world. During Britten's successful career, practically every other British composer was suppressed, not allowed to have a real success. As soon as he died they let Tippett have a little one late—too late to amount to anything—but now they've handed over the whole system of privilege to Max Davies.[29] The entire diplomatic establishment's behind that—as well as the trained critics. Early in Britten's career, Henry Barraud[30] was musical head of the French Radio and told me: "People are always asking me if I get pressure from the Soviet government, but I only hear from them maybe once in six months or a year. But not a week goes by without my getting a letter from the British Embassy demanding that I play certain works by Benjamin Britten!" [*laughs*]

PD   I've heard you on this subject before, and I think you oversimplify.

VT   I'm sure I do. [*laughs*] But from my position here, Max Davies has got it made.

---

29. Sir Michael Tippett (1905–98); Sir Peter Maxwell Davies (1934–). Davies was appointed Master of the Queen's Music in 2004, twenty-three years after Thomson made this assertion.

30. Henry Barraud (1900–1997) was head of music for Radiodiffusion Française after World War II and director of the Programme National during the years 1948–65.

Part Five

Performers

Chapter Eleven

Leontyne Price

Interview with Peter Dickinson, New York City, May 14, 1981

Introduction

Leontyne Price, one of the leading international sopranos of her generation, was born in Laurel, Mississippi, in 1927. After studying at Juilliard, she attracted attention in 1952 when Virgil Thomson chose her for the revival of his opera *Four Saints in Three Acts* on Broadway. The following year she starred as Bess in Gershwin's *Porgy and Bess* at the Ziegfeld Theater, and a two-year world tour followed. Her future stature as a great Verdi performer became clear when she sang Aida at San Francisco, Vienna, Covent Garden, and La Scala. Her Metropolitan Opera debut was in 1961 as Leonora in *Il trovatore*. She recalls in detail here her experiences as Cleopatra in Barber's opera written for the opening of the new Metropolitan Opera at Lincoln Center in 1966. Her repertoire included Monteverdi, Handel, Mozart, and Puccini, but she returned to Verdi for her final appearance as Aida in 1985.

Rudolf Bing, general manager of the Met, wanted Price to open the new opera house with a new American opera. Interviewed as she arrived on opening night, September 16, 1966, Price said she was grateful for the privilege and the honor and went on: "I'm anything but calm. I'm exhilarated beyond belief and excited completely out of my skin!" She was pleased that her hometown could be connected to the broadcast—and, of course, she sang magnificently, with countless high notes delivered with total assurance.[1]

---

1. The *Bell Telephone Hour* presented the film *The New Met: Count Down to Curtain* in September 1966, which included interviews with Rudolf Bing, Franco Zeffirelli, and Price.

Interview

By Permission of Leontyne Price

LP   I consider myself very fortunate to have known a composer of Samuel
Barber's magnitude and for him to have written things for me. I'm exhilarated beyond belief to know that I am one of those rare creatures who
have had the privilege of having a composer write not only an opera centered around my own instrument but also a cycle of songs.[2] Beginning in
those early days in the 1950s I considered myself a very devoted friend of
Sam's, as I called him affectionately, which I think is as important for a
singer and a composer as it would be for a singer and a conductor. I had
a sort of strange, special *marriage* with Sam. I still do because as long as I
can sing, there will always be regular performances of his compositions.

My beloved teacher Florence Page Kimball[3] was a great friend of Samuel
Barber's, as was another beloved friend, Nicholas Nabokov.[4] When I was
a student at Juilliard there was a great deal of focus through him and
Virgil Thomson on this instrument of mine, thank God! I met Samuel
Barber, Henri Sauguet, Francis Poulenc—so many contemporary composers it really blew my mind—and I began to learn a lot of compositions. Almost instantly, there was this affinity for Barber's music, the way
it sort of embraces my instrument, as does Verdi and some Mozart and
Strauss. It's the same kind of thing. And there was an invitation from the
Library of Congress to do a premiere with him of the *Hermit Songs,* which
was really the first major exposure I'd had with him.[5] He was an exquisite
pianist, and he was a wonderful vocalist too, a light lyric baritone, and
could always sing to you what he wanted. He could sing the phrases himself and play at the same time, which I thought was ambidextrous at its
best! And, treading where angels fear to tread, I said, "Look, why don't
we team up?" [*laughs*] I was having a terrible case of stage fright—well
who doesn't?—and we did it with great success. There was the usual musical grapevine interest in my debut in Town Hall because the word was

---

2. *Despite and Still,* op. 41 (1968).

3. Florence Page Kimball (1890–1977) studied voice with Marcella Sembrich and succeeded her as a faculty member at the Juilliard Graduate School in 1927. She remained
on the faculty until her retirement in 1975.

4. Nicholas Nabokov (1903–78), Russian American composer, studied in St. Petersburg, Berlin, and Paris, where he was commissioned by Diaghilev to write a ballet. Moved
to the United States in 1933.

5. *Hermit Songs,* op. 29 (1953), Coolidge Auditorium, Library of Congress, October 30,
1953, with works by Poulenc and Sauguet also on the program.

beginning to spread—thank goodness! I was graduating from *Porgy and Bess,* bridging the gap between folk opera and the main event. In 1954 my Town Hall debut was scheduled. And I said: "You're not going to let me down now. You're going to play for me on my Town Hall debut. I mean, we've rehearsed it, why not play it with me?" And that's the first time anyone has had two pianists in one concert! [*laughs*] So my Town Hall debut was with Samuel Barber at the piano in his own composition. We were both scared out of our wits before in the wings. But it went very well, and the friendship just grew and grew. I think to date there are only two compositions of his for the voice that I have not sung, songs especially for male voice—the ones written for Dietrich Fischer-Dieskau[6] and *Andromache's Farewell.*[7] He did a wonderful arrangement of part of the *Antony and Cleopatra* score—the kernel of Cleopatra's music, which, I think, is the most beautifully written on earth. And I have performed it, and still do, with orchestra and with glorious success. A few seasons ago there was a performance with Zubin Mehta and the New York Philharmonic of *The Death of Cleopatra,* and Sam was able to come out and take a bow for I can't tell you how long. The music was so beautifully played, which made me extremely happy because it's such a stunning opera.

PD   Can you cast your mind back to when you first worked with him and he was playing the piano for you in his own music? What did he ask you to do? What was he looking for?

LP   It wasn't so much what he asked me to do as that he liked the sound of my instrument. It fit his music and went wherever his phrases went. It's something you don't take a pencil and paper to; it's chemistry, like love, like sex, very intimate relationships. In the studio with Miss Kimball he might have an idea of a variation in tempo from the time when he wrote it. Before publication he might want to try out something in one or two keys because the published key might be a different range. So I would do several versions for him. All the technical things involved were no problem. He liked to have rehearsals to find out the flow of the poem, with the accent on exactly what he wanted expressively. Phrase that way to make a *legato,* going up, over, or through—that kind of thing, strictly from the point of view of the poetry. It was just one of those wonderful relationships. And I almost always did what he wanted as soon as I'd learned the song.

---

6. *Three Songs,* op. 45 (1972); Dietrich Fischer-Dieskau (1925–), widely celebrated German baritone.

7. *Andromache's Farewell,* op. 39, for soprano and orchestra (1962), premiered by Martina Arroyo, with the New York Philharmonic/Schippers, in Philharmonic Hall, April 4–7, 1963.

PD   How did it compare with working with an accompanist for lieder recitals?

LP   Well, I don't have an accompanist. I have a fellow artist, namely David Garvey, and that is my longest and most successful collaboration. He also has a great affinity for Barber's music and got firsthand all the personal things Sam had to say about it. Since I've never worked with another, I always have close relationships and I keep them forever. This is our twenty-fourth season, so all the Barber I've done has been with David Garvey.

PD   I know what you mean, and I wasn't suggesting an accompanist wasn't a fellow artist, but was Barber different from a pianist who is not a composer? Is there something special when it's composer at the keyboard?

LP   I think so—it's very special. He made me feel rather mother-henny because he was always so petrified. I felt like Joan of Arc! [*laughs*] Once he was there, it's like he was composing again. It was that kind of personal thing.

PD   What do you think is American about his music?

LP   I think Sam Barber is our Monet.[8] I said that once in an interview and he loved it. I think he's a musician's composer, a romantic composer, and an extremely vocal composer. He's one of the greatest composers of our time. And being American is, of course, wonderful, but it's more international. Think of the blues and reds in Monet, particularly the blues. There must be a thousand kinds of blues in Monet, without the sharp steeliness of a Van Gogh but with the lusciousness and fluidity! That's what I think of Sam's music. And he liked that. He sent me a lovely bouquet of anemones saying "thank you, my darling," which was very nice. I think his music has an outreach that is not totally American.

PD   You talked about him being a musician's artist. But he was a very popular composer—he died leaving a million dollars!

LP   Yes, he was very successful. That's because he wrote from feelings. At the same time, he had an extraordinary mind, and he did not write to show off to his colleagues or his peers. He wrote out of emotion, which I think makes a great artist. It was not antiseptic. Orchestras love to play his music because it is mentally challenging, you're never bored, and for the singer it's a challenge, but the end product is so rewarding and so terribly vocal that you can't wait to pick up another piece of his. It's that quality that makes his music popular. It falls intellectually to the mind and beautifully on the ear, which is a rare combination.

PD   Tell me about his wit or other things that were characteristic.

---

8. Claude Monet (1840–1926), French impressionist painter.

LP   He had a very sharp wit that could be biting, depending on his mood. He was a very complex gentleman who wrote heart-rending music. I would like to think he was a happy man, but I think he was greatly saddened after *Antony and Cleopatra*.[9] That was something that affected him in a negative way. I think he recovered to an extent, but I do not agree with everyone that it was a fiasco. The importance of the occasion was not taken seriously enough by his fellow artists.

PD   How did you work on *Antony?* Did you get it bit by bit?

LP   Yes, right here at this piano. Sam would come with a page; my house-keeper would be busy fixing a type of chicken he liked, and we would be busy working at it.

I have one of the first pages—a collector's item. I'm having it framed. He would call often to see how it was going, and I would ask if I could sing it for him.

When I visited him in hospital I'd sing "Give Me Some Music" [*sings*][10] and he'd say, "I've got to get out of here and write a new cycle for you." I would never say goodbye to him. I would sing him something on the phone. This is the way we did *A and C* as I would call it [*laughs*] when we were working on it. That was a very harassing experience for him. We were all on the spot. I said, "With this kind of responsibility I just can't catch a common cold all year," and I lived like a nun. It was that kind of tightrope. There was the extra complexity of moving into a new house, new mechanism, new opera, new everything. It didn't go smoothly.[11]

PD   *Antony and Cleopatra* may have run into trouble because it was a very elaborate production, and it may have been over-publicized because of the new Lincoln Center.

LP   Not over-publicized. It was a great American event, so it couldn't be over-publicized.[12] It was also the complexity of moving an entire institution from one home to another. The mechanism of moving the people who

---

9. *Antony and Cleopatra*, op. 40 (1966, revised 1974); commissioned for the opening of the new Metropolitan Opera House on September 16, 1966. "Everything Fine at the New Met but the Opera," *The Times* (London), September 19, 1966.

10. From *Antony and Cleopatra*, act 1, scene 3.

11. In the *Bell Telephone Hour* film Rudolf Bing, general manager of the Met, explained that there were staggering problems in mounting four new productions in nine days: "I don't think I visualised the hell it would be."

12. In the *Bell Telephone Hour* film, Price, while being made up, said: "It has to be a massive mammoth production to lend itself to this score, which I think is superb . . . an opera score of great grandeur . . . requires get-up-and-go!"

work to make the whole house go is like moving yourself from one apartment to another. It takes time to find your way around. But to do all that with a new opera was complex, with so many things to do at once that were impossible in the time. But we were able to do nine or ten performances, and it got better as it went along.

The first night itself, I can testify, was a [hair-raising] experience for me. I had a three-minute cue, and I was locked in the pyramid after the first aria! [*laughs*] I could see my life and my next cue going down the drain in the pitch dark because something mechanical didn't open up at the right time. But I must say—and there's no business like show business—I simply kept singing in the pyramid. [*laughs*] I'll be heard no matter what! [*laughs*] There have been a lot of jokes about that afterward. And I kept singing through to the next cue. I could see Thomas Schippers; his life went straight before his face because there was no way in the world I could make that cue.[13] I was to be dressed inside the pyramid for the next costume, and I just simply said, "Zip this one back up whether it fits or not. I'll keep singing and just go out." And that's what I did. It was because of the stage, which was so intricate in the new Met, that various things did not gel. There was a barge—a sensational idea of Franco Zeffirelli's—that worked sometimes and sometimes it didn't.[14] But being on it, [*laughs*] it seemed a much longer distance from freedom than I would like to think about in the middle of the night in my dreams from time to time. But I was able to develop a sense of humor about it. I don't think Sam ever did, really.

PD   Why did you have to go inside the pyramid? What were you doing there?

LP   It was like a change of scene, to make another atmosphere, and it was so fascinatingly done by Zeffirelli that it just looked like Cleopatra was swallowed by the pyramid. Don't ask me why; I don't know. But it was very effective from out front—just not from where I was! [*laughs*][15]

PD   One thing that's clear from our interviews is that Barber had very close associations with performers and chose them with particular care. Composers also need conductors, and Thomas Schippers was very interested in Barber's music, wasn't he?

---

13. Thomas Schippers (1930–77), prominent American conductor. According to the *Bell Telephone Hour* film, at the dress rehearsal, which included an audience, the pyramid was stuck and wouldn't move. Proceedings had to be stopped, and the curtain was brought down. Price said, "I'll never get out of here with my life, I know it!" The mechanism also failed on the first night, but the pyramid had moved out of sight.

14. The *Bell Telephone Hour* film shows that Zeffirelli drove the production and stage crews to the limit and well beyond. Rudolf Bing had to contend with all this as well as with a threatened orchestra strike.

15. The scene change was from Alexandria to Rome.

LP   He was quite a devotee of Barber's music and very much involved with the composing of it at firsthand, as I was. So it made a special flavor for his conducting, and he knew everything absolutely cold. It was very exciting when we'd done a recording of the excerpts.

PD   Did you see the Juilliard production in 1974?[16]

LP   Yes, I did. I was sitting with Barber at the time. We just sat there and wrung three or four handkerchiefs together. It was so beautiful. He was so happy that day and so was I—it was a lovely performance.

PD   That was after Menotti had helped.

LP   Well, he did it. He produced it for the Juilliard School.

PD   So we shouldn't exaggerate the disappointment at the Met in view of this later production?

LP   I'm not, even though I was not personally involved in it.

AJ[17]   During the rehearsals for *Antony and Cleopatra,* did you have any intimations of the fiasco that was ahead?

LP   I don't think it was a fiasco. I've never been in a fiasco. I have a winning streak in me! [*laughs*] I just thought: too many things were going on at once—the absolute mechanics of moving an entire institution to another place. That's what led to a great deal of difficulty, not just for *Antony and Cleopatra* but also for other productions later.

I thought: I am going to sing Sam's music the best I can, in the middle of whatever chaos that cannot be remedied. I will not let his music be unheard. It is the most beautiful music ever written; it fits my voice like a glove, and whatever happens I will not shut up my mouth. At the dress rehearsals I saw this was on my shoulders as a *protagonista,* and opera is singing. I saw no other thing to do.

PD   Have you noticed a different response to his music in different countries where you've performed?

---

16. The revival was given by the American Opera Center at the Juilliard School on February 6–10, 1975. James Conlon conducted and Esther Hinds sang Cleopatra—and again at the Spoleto Festivals in Italy and Charleston, South Carolina, in 1983. See Andrew Porter, "Antony's Second Chance," in *Music of Three Seasons: 1974–1977* (New York: Farrar, Straus and Giroux, 1978), 97–102, for a balanced assessment of the situation from one of the most experienced opera critics. He concludes: "I suspect that if the opera is revived a century or so hence, directors of the future will want to combine both scores in new arrangements . . . reinstating valued passages which the composer himself cut but retaining passages he strengthened by recomposition" (102).

17. Arthur Johnson.

LP   Well, I always promised Sam, even in recitals in the United States, to have the printed texts of his works—the poetry. I use a duplicate in German of the English texts, so it makes it easier for everybody. He was very clinical about that kind of thing and would say, "If you can't do it, I'll have it done." That was one of the rules.

PD   Do you remember anything else like that, where he had an absolute conviction that something should happen and was prepared to insist on it?

LP   Diction: he worked very much with the poem, which he liked to hear. It was always exemplary from a vocal point of view. He was very much involved, very patient. He could always find the time to come to rehearsals, and he was just a stickler for what's best, a perfectionist in every area—with orchestras too. When Mehta was doing the *Third Essay* written for the New York Philharmonic, I know he was present at all the rehearsals, from the first stages until the curtain went up.

PD   Have you any favorite instrumental pieces?

LP   The *Adagio for Strings* I'd like played at my funeral. Just play it at my funeral. There's nothing ever written like it.

PD   Is that because you associate it with the Kennedy funeral?

LP   No, I just associate it with Sam as the most beautiful thing he's written. I mean, the strings just kill you. It tears you apart. No, it just has to do with my own idea. I didn't even know it was played at Kennedy's funeral.

PD   People have different responses, but what they are agreed about is the intensity of the piece.

LP   That's what I'm getting at. Most moving. Unforgettable, as is *Knoxville: Summer of 1915*. As a southerner, it expresses everything I know about my roots and about my Mum and Daddy and my hometown. Eleanor Steber commissioned it, and I'm a very great admirer of hers—a beautiful rendition.

AJ   It's interesting that Barber, who was not from the South, wrote *Knoxville,* which is so appropriate and so understandable to a southerner.

LP   There's no cataloging a great artist. It is delving into the beauty of the Agee poem and setting it right to music. You can smell the South in it.

AJ   Somebody once said to me that you really have to be an American to appreciate *Knoxville.*

LP   I don't agree at all. *Knoxville* is like my own folklore. It is an American product of the soil, the wonder of my country presented so that others can understand it too. It's like being a tourist. It's not as if you're going to stay there forever, but you can get a flavor. English history is one of my hobbies, but I would never be able to be British, but there is something about the continuity of your history that fascinates me. So I can learn as much as I can, absorb it, and appreciate it. I feel the same way an audience of any other culture would about *Knoxville*.

AJ   There are very strong, nostalgic visual images in the text.

LP   Totally—it's like a painting, and I think he set it perfectly. You can hear the streetcar, the horns, and everything; you can smell the strawberries. As always, we southerners would lie on quilts on the grass at night and hear all those strange noises of summer.

PD   Is it an American way of setting words to music? Does it need American inflections?

LP   It is our kind of English, not the bravura Oxford approach. I've been told I sound like a young person. That's because I have this image already; it's in my blood, my roots. Maybe a type of American know-how is required. I wouldn't say it can't be sung by someone else, but it might help to make it what it should be.

PD   Was Barber the last of the romantics?

LP   I think Ned Rorem can come from the heart as well. Lee Hoiby, who studied a bit with Barber, is a very vocal writer. Howard Swanson is not quite appreciated enough. Argento's a fine writer. Carlyle Floyd writes beautifully. There are some.[18]

---

18. Ned Rorem (1923–); Lee Hoiby (1926–); Howard Swanson (1907–78); Dominick Argento (1927–); Carlisle Floyd (1926–).

Chapter Twelve

John Browning

Interview with Peter Dickinson, New York City, May 13, 1981

Introduction

John Browning (1933–2003) was a prominent American pianist who made his first appearance at age ten in Denver, Colorado, where he was born. After study in Los Angeles, he went to the Juilliard School of Music as a pupil of Rosina Lhévinne.[1] He won several awards and made his debut with the New York Philharmonic under Dmitri Mitropoulos in 1956—Barber was at that concert.[2] Browning was subsequently in demand internationally and toured the USSR in 1965.

He was mostly involved with the standard repertoire, from Mozart to Rachmaninov, but he also recorded the Prokofiev concertos and made a particular impact with the Barber Piano Concerto when he premiered it with the Boston Symphony Orchestra under Erich Leinsdorf at Lincoln Center on September 24, 1962.[3] The concerto was commissioned for the opening of the new Philharmonic Hall. Browning played it 50 times in its first two seasons and by 1969 had chalked up almost 150 performances. The concerto gained Barber his second Pulitzer Prize and a Music Critics Circle Award. Browning made two recordings and also accompanied the complete songs of Barber with Cheryl Studer and Thomas Hampson.[4] Browning's obituary in *The Times* focused on his role in launching "one of the most popular . . . of the select body of distinguished piano concertos composed since World War II."[5]

---

1. Rosina Lhévinne (1880–1976), American pianist born in Kiev, one of the great teachers of the era, who taught at Juilliard from 1924 until shortly before she died.

2. Dmitri Mitropolous (1889–1965), Greek-born American conductor who directed the New York Philharmonic from 1949 to 1957 and conducted the premiere of *Vanessa* at the Metropolitan Opera on January 15, 1958.

3. Erich Leinsdorf (1912–93), Austrian-born American conductor.

4. Barber, Piano Concerto, Cleveland Orchestra/Szell, SONY SMK 89751 (1964); St. Louis Symphony/Slatkin, RCA RD60732 (1991); *Samuel Barber: The Songs*, Cheryl Studer, Thomas Hampson, John Browning, Emerson String Quartet, Deutsche Grammophon 435 867–2 (1994).

5. Obituary, *The Times* (London), March 7, 2003.

Interview

By Permission of Elizabeth B. Witchey

JB   Sam and I met in 1956. I was making my debut with Mitropoulos and the New York Philharmonic, and his *Medea's Meditation and Dance of Vengeance* was being premiered. And then Schirmer's commissioned the Piano Concerto and Sam called me and said, "Do you want to do it?" and I said, "Of course. I would be very honored." I didn't get the last movement until about ten days before the premiere, so I was practicing about fifteen hours a day trying to get it memorized because it's frightfully difficult.

PD   What discussions did you have with Sam Barber about the kind of music it might be? Did he come to you with sketches?

JB   Sam had a very interesting way of writing for artists. He would have any of us for whom he was writing a work come up to the country house at Mt. Kisco and play through everything we knew for three, four, or five days. Mr. Horowitz did it, Miss Price did it, I did it.[6] And he would get a feel of what he thought our strong points were. For example, Horowitz taught him a tremendous amount about the sostenuto pedal, the middle pedal, and he began to use that a great deal. I brought up things my teacher Rosina Lhévinne had told me about flutter pedals and dividing runs two octaves apart instead of one, which makes a much bigger sound. So, in a way, we all contributed in our fashion to ideas he then went with. For example, he ended the first draft of the first movement *pianissimo*, and both Mr. Leinsdorf and I, in hearing it, thought: "Maybe we could suggest that it might end *fortissimo* so the slow movement would come out of nowhere." And Sam was always wonderful in that way; he always listened to the performer, and if he hadn't wanted to change it he wouldn't have, but he thought "it's a good idea," so he did.

PD   Were there other places like that?

JB   There were some passages in the last movement that were almost unplayable, particularly at the tempo that it goes. And I said: "Sam, I just cannot seem to get through them. Can't we do short cuts? I think it will be just as effective." And he said: "Let's take it over to Mr. Horowitz. If he says it can't be done, then it can't be done." And we took it over.

---

6. Vladimir Horowitz (1903–89), Russian-born pianist who settled in the United States in 1928. He played the sonata in Havana, Cuba, on December 9, 1949, then at a private hearing at Schirmer's on January 4, 1950; but the official premiere was at Constitution Hall in Washington DC, on January 11, 1950. It received rave notices in the United States. Horowitz recorded it on May 15, 1950: Victor DM-1466, later RCA.

Mr. Horowitz said: "Sam, I'm afraid John is right. It cannot be played at that tempo." [*laughs*]

PD   When you went to play to him, what sort of pieces did you play? Did you play his own sonata?

JB   No. He had heard me play that. I played everything else—I played lots of Chopin, Debussy, Bach, Beethoven—anything.

PD   Any Schoenberg or anything like that?

JB   No. He wasn't very interested. He did use the twelve-tone technique, but only as a device.

PD   I read that somebody who went to interview him when he was working on the Piano Concerto found the Schoenberg Piano Concerto score on his piano.[7]

JB   I'm sure he consulted a great many other concerti. He never told me which ones, so I don't really know. But it would be logical if you're writing a contemporary concerto, even though you don't want to write like Schoenberg, to see what he had done.

PD   Do you know the *Excursions*?[8]

JB   Yes. I played them. I haven't kept them in my repertory because, although they're very fascinating pieces, they don't seem to have an audience success in the way the sonata does. So it just seems somehow the sonata and the concerto have been what I've played the most.

PD   Could you be more specific?

JB   I find them fascinating in the same way the Copland sonata [1941] has not achieved the kind of performance it should because it ends so softly and the audience just doesn't get it.

PD   And one of the characteristics of Barber was that he understood so well what would go?

JB   Yes. He wrote for the public. He was very conscious of public reaction, and he wanted things to be theatrically successful.[9] Of course, *Antony* was not, but I think with time we have realized that it was far more the direction and the production that was at fault and not the music.

---

7. John Ardoin, "Samuel Barber at Capricorn," *Musical America* (March 1960): 4, 5, 46.

8. *Four Excursions*, op. 20 (1942–44).

9. As early as 1935 Barber was reported as saying: "My aim is to write good music that will be comprehensible to as many people as possible, instead of music heard only by small snobbish musical societies in the larger cities." Barbara B. Heyman, *Samuel Barber: The Composer and His Music* (New York: Oxford University Press, 1992), 130.

PD   He's sometimes described as a conservative composer. What kind of a composer does that make him?

JB   I think, perhaps like a good performer, a good composer wants a work to succeed—just as we try to make the performance of a work as successful as possible. Now, there have been composers whom we have called "ivory tower" composers who, it seemed to us, were not writing with the public in mind—people like John Cage.[10] I think in the case of Barber and certainly Britten, these were men who cannot be viewed as contemporary; they must be viewed as we would view Bach or Rachmaninov, who was certainly not a twentieth-century composer. It doesn't matter when he wrote. It just doesn't matter. The music is of its own genre. And I think Sam is very much the same way. Certainly, there were contemporary things, but I think Sam achieved a rather eclectic sound—he sounds actually less American than, say, Copland. And yet it was Nadia Boulanger who taught Copland and many other Americans, but Sam never worked with Madame Boulanger.

PD   Does it matter that he doesn't seem to be American—or perhaps he does to you?

JB   I think that in some of the early works like *Knoxville,* where the poetry was very clearly American, then the sound was more so. As he went on I think the later works became far more Scriabin-ish, far more into a kind of European sound, not that wide-open spaced sound we think of as being American.

PD   What is the Barber sound?

JB   I think the one thing that stands out is the absolutely superb mastery of counterpoint. Really, Sam was a contrapuntal composer. When one looks at the fugue of the sonata, I do not know of another piano fugue as successful since the Brahms *Handel Variations* or as well written. He studied Bach every day, and he was so comfortable in these forms that they were a natural language. One had the feeling that he was every bit as comfortable with a four-part fugue as Bach was, that he could have written it down like a good crossword puzzle, in ink! That kind of security. I think later on particularly the harmonies were very turn of the century—very Russian almost—but with functional basses. As I say, Sam was perfectly capable of writing twelve tone or dissonance if he wanted to. He always said, "I never want to get trapped in a form or a method."

---

10. John Cage (1912–92), influential American avant-garde figure. See Peter Dickinson, *CageTalk: Dialogues with and about John Cage* (Rochester, NY: University of Rochester Press, 2006).

PD　　　What sort of a person was he?

JB　　　He was a very complicated man. He had a very dry wit. He could be very
　　　　　aloof and very snobbish; he could also be very "old shoe" and very com-
　　　　　fortable. He loved to have prominent friends very well placed, but he did
　　　　　not use them in a bad way at all. Of course, he and Gian Carlo Menotti
　　　　　had a long association for well over thirty years. I think Sam could be
　　　　　very difficult, at the same time very loyal: he was wonderful to me, he was
　　　　　wonderful to Miss Price. He stood by his artists, if that makes sense. He
　　　　　was an extremely intellectual man; he read constantly; he was fluent in
　　　　　German, French, Italian, Spanish—absolutely fluent. He was truly a very
　　　　　cultivated man. He, in a sense I think, almost thought of himself as more
　　　　　European, oddly enough, because he had lived a great deal in Europe,
　　　　　with the house in Santa Cristina in the Dolomites. He loved Europe, the
　　　　　boats trips of the old days, the European atmosphere. He was a man who
　　　　　became increasingly irritated by the square, modern buildings. He would
　　　　　have been much happier in a nineteenth-century house.

AJ[11]　It's interesting that he moved to Fifth Avenue in the end.

JB　　　Yes. Well, he had a horrible apartment on 66th Street, which he thought
　　　　　was a very chic building, but it was just an ugly apartment—particularly
　　　　　after the sale of the house, Capricorn, at Mt. Kisco, which broke his
　　　　　heart. We urged him to just go and buy a spiffy Fifth Avenue apartment
　　　　　with nice high ceilings and moldings, and he did. I think he was very
　　　　　happy there.[12]

PD　　　Tell me about the swimming pool and the Piano Concerto.

JB　　　Schirmer's asked Sam what he wanted in the way of commission, and he
　　　　　said, "I just want a swimming pool." So the swimming pool became the
　　　　　prize for having written a good piano concerto!

PD　　　Of course, he had a marvelous relationship with Schirmer over the years.

JB　　　Yes, he was one of the very few people who was kept on a retainer by
　　　　　Schirmer, in a way Copland and Bernstein and people like that had been
　　　　　kept on retainers whether they write or not. Don't ask me the system, but
　　　　　it seems to work! There is some way in which they feel that, for example
　　　　　with the *Adagio,* which made a great deal of money, the publishers would
　　　　　then parcel out some of that money to young, struggling composers who
　　　　　needed a bit of help.

---

11. Arthur Johnson.
12. 200 E. 66th Street (1973–75), then 907 5th Avenue.

PD   Some of his music is highly dramatic—a piece like *The Lovers.*

JB   I did the Piano Concerto at the premiere of *The Lovers.* We started with the concerto.[13]

PD   Do you feel that behind his music there is a turbulence, a kind of emotional instability that gave it a driving force?

JB   Emotional instability? No. I wouldn't say that; it was never my feeling. Certainly, in much of the later music there's a kind of yearning, as in some of the Brahms intermezzi, for things that perhaps he had not had, emotional feelings that had never been realized.

PD   Was he adjusted to being gay? I imagine he wouldn't have liked the word because his generation often didn't.

JB   He was, as far as I know, very well adjusted to it. He came, of course, from a period when it was not talked about very much, and he always had the extraordinary ability to make the best possible friends so that he was socially invulnerable—people like Mary Curtis Bok. I think people of that generation did it that way. You made yourself socially so impeccable that nobody could say anything. I think he was deeply in love with Gian Carlo, and I think he remained so until the end of his life. I think it was an absolute one-person relationship in very much the way Peter Pears and Benjamin Britten were.

PD   With a lot of musical spin-off, too, because Gian Carlo introduced him to Italy and possibly brought Barber to opera.

JB   Oh, I think so. Certainly, Sam felt safe whenever Gian Carlo was producing or directing. And, of course, he made the mistake of not having Gian Carlo do the original *Antony.* Franco Zeffirelli simply did not know what he was doing. I think Sam was deeply hurt by the failure because it was the opening of the new Met, and therefore every critic from all over the world was there—and it was a fiasco. I think he never really recovered from that—and then the breakup of the relationship and the sale of the house. I think those three things broke his heart. So I don't think his last twelve or thirteen years were happy at all. Certainly, they were not productive.

PD   The *Third Essay* is now on record.[14] It's quite a strong piece.

---

13. Philadelphia Orchestra/Ormandy, September 22, 1971.
14. *Third Essay for Orchestra,* op. 47 (1978), premiered on September 14, 1978, by the New York Philharmonic under Zubin Mehta.

JB   It's a strong piece. It took a little doing to get it the right length, but that was one of the few things he wrote between 1970 and 1980.[15]

In trying to think back over *Antony and Cleopatra*, Sam was talked into using Zeffirelli by the management of the Met, which was a great mistake. Of course, at that time Zeffirelli was very chic. But as Suso d'Amico in Rome used to say: "Zeffirelli is extremely good with the thirteenth production of *Rigoletto* or something, but he really cannot do an original production."[16]

PD   It was one thing to tart up the classics but another thing to start from scratch?

JB   Right. And then all the unions struck just weeks before. The turntable, which was designed for the elephant or whatever, broke. All the problems of a new house—there was no backup board, only an electronic lighting board. In that respect, everything that could go wrong with the house and with the production went wrong. I don't think anybody wanted it to be a disaster. I think I have to place the majority of the blame on Zeffirelli because he went way over budget, and I think he did not really know how to handle Sam's music. The other thing is that *Antony and Cleopatra* is a very difficult work. It's not a true love relationship, it's not a true war play, it's the most difficult of all the Shakespeare works to put into operatic form. And again Sam had done an excellent version of his own—and then he copped out to Zeffirelli, who wanted 5 percent to do the libretto. And the changes Zeffirelli made were all catastrophic.

PD   We don't need to leave it on an unhappy note because the Juilliard 1974 production . . .

JB   Was stunning and cost eighteen thousand, if I'm not mistaken, whereas the original Met production cost well over a million! And unnecessary— every bit of copper tubing in the city of New York was used. Poor Miss Price was trapped in this Sphinx that was rolling around the stage—she lost a whole scene. There was a terrible feeling in the house all the way through the production that "we are watching a failure."

PD   Copland's orchestral *Connotations* for the new Philharmonic Hall in 1962 wasn't exactly a smash hit either?

---

15. See Heyman, *Samuel Barber: The Composer and His Music.*

16. Suso Cecchi d'Amico (1914–), Italian screenwriter who worked with Zeffirelli. She and Barber shared an enthusiasm for James Joyce, and Barber dedicated two of his Joyce songs (*Three Songs*, op. 10) to her and her brother.

JB   No. Also I think Sam tended to write one work. He wrote one con-
      certo for piano, one cello concerto; I think his best writing in opera
      went into *Vanessa*. I think what *Antony* does reflect is the breakup of
      the relationship between him and Menotti, and in that sense you might
      say that Sam was letting himself be persuaded to do things that came out
      of a certain kind of emotional insecurity.

PD   Gian Carlo said they were reconciled.

JB   Yes, they were reconciled, but it was not the way Sam wanted to spend
      his last years. I talked to Gian Carlo about this after Sam's death, and he
      kept saying, "Well, we just couldn't get along." Maybe two composers,
      like two pianists—very dangerous. I think in some ways there may have
      been some envy because Gian Carlo was a theater person but not a great
      composer. I mean, the theater pieces like *The Consul* [1950] and *Amahl*
      [1951], there's wonderful music in them, but in terms of compositional
      technique I don't think you can put the two in the same category at all.
      And I've always wondered if Gian Carlo just couldn't handle that.

PD   Menotti couldn't handle it? That's interesting, because I wondered if Bar-
      ber was somewhat jealous perhaps of Menotti's operatic successes after
      World War II.

JB   Of course, we can't get away from the Schippers relationship. It started
      a long time before I knew Sam; it gradually started going on the rocks.
      Gian Carlo was always more interested in younger men. I don't think
      Sam cared, really. He was attracted by them, but he was truly married to
      Gian Carlo. There's absolutely no question about it. I don't think Gian
      Carlo felt quite the same thing. But I don't think we'll ever know the
      whole story.[17]

      In Sam's composing, he certainly had very deep, very strong emotions,
      but he was not particularly forceful. He could be very caustic from time
      to time, but you did not get the feeling of a tremendously high-powered,
      forceful man. He worked very slowly, the whole output is forty-eight
      opuses. He was a very careful worker, but I would not say that he was
      driven. He had enough security financially that he did not have to crank
      out works to make ends meet.

---

17. Schippers told John Gruen about the complexities of these relationships: "no one
will be able to explain them to anyone." Gruen, *Menotti: A Biography* (New York: Macmillan, 1978), 140–41.

PD   I was about to speculate about the *Adagio* because of its incredible popularity. For example, Virgil Thomson has said it's a love scene; Leontyne Price thinks it's about death. I'm not suggesting something as naïve as a program, but why has it become a classic?

JB   I really can't explain that. For example, it was played constantly after the Kennedy assassination.[18] Why it? We heard it day and night. When we played some music for Sam in the hospital, we did the *Summer Music* and I played some Chopin mazurkas—I couldn't get through anything of his on an upright—and then the string quartet played the *Adagio,* and of course everybody in the room broke up—we could hardly hang on to ourselves. So, obviously, it does have that effect, and I can't tell you what it is. I don't think it has to do with death. It's very Bachian in a way—the tremendous admiration Sam had for Bach comes out, I think, very strongly.[19] And yet there's this tremendously lush texture—and I think it is that lushness that is perhaps the word I was searching for in the overall harmonic writing; it's very, very lush.

PD   It sometimes looks back to Palestrina with a modal flavor?

JB   I think, of all contemporary American composers, Sam was closest in his writing to the vocal style because his aunt had been the great opera singer Louise Homer, and he was very close to "Aunt Lulu," as he called her, and I think there's an innate lyricism in no matter what instrument he wrote for, there's always that feeling of vocal line. He was himself a fine singer. I think that, almost more than anything else, is what perhaps characterizes his music for me. At all times the vocal persuasiveness is there, which so many contemporary composers have not given us.

[In more casual conversation, Browning moved to Anglo-American musical relations, what he called "the Anglo-American problem."]

---

18. According to Nathan Broder: "Somewhat to the composer's dismay, the *Adagio for Strings* has accumulated a funereal tinge. It was broadcast from New York a few minutes after the news of President Roosevelt's death [1945]; it was performed in England shortly thereafter to commemorate the same event; in South Africa on the passing of Jan Christian Smuts [1950], and in Cincinnati, Ohio, in memory of Senator Robert Taft [1953]." Broder, *Samuel Barber* (New York: G. Schirmer, 1954), 74n1.

19. Barber wrote *Mutations from Bach for Brass Choir and Timpani* (1967) drawing on the hymn "Christe du lamm Gottes," in various versions by Bach.

JB   Like so many other Anglo-American things, why don't Americans like
      Delius very much? Why didn't Sam like Britten? Why didn't Britten like
      Sam's music all that much? Who knows? Sometimes I think we're just too
      much of a family, with all the problems. [*laughs*] But it seems to run that
      way with British music. . . . I mean, *Peter Grimes* is a masterpiece, and it
      took a long time to get that production at the Met.[20]

      I don't know why. It all seems very silly to me.

---

20. *Peter Grimes* (1945) was produced at the Met on February 12, 1948, and has been
seen there seventy times since. In Peter Pears, *Travel Diaries 1936–1978*, ed. Philip Reed
(Woodbridge, Suffolk: Boydell, 1995), he described his visit to the Met to sing Aschen-
bach in Britten's *Death in Venice* in 1974. While there, he went to a performance of Berg's
Wozzeck with the American music administrator and publisher Betty Bean, but they didn't
like the work. His diary entry concluded: "Give me *Albert Herring* every time. We left after
the second act. Met Sam Barber there" (191). Unlike the reference to Copland on the
same page, there was no footnote about Barber. That was probably the only occasion on
which either Britten or Pears met Barber. The four published volumes of Britten's diaries
make no mention of Barber. See also Daniel Felsenfeld, *Britten and Barber: Their Lives and
Their Music* (Pompton Plains, NJ: Amadeus, 2005).

Chapter Thirteen

Robert White

Interview with Arthur Johnson, London, February 1981

Introduction

Robert White (1936–), tenor and teacher, was born in New York City. He studied with Nadia Boulanger at Fontainebleau and was a soloist in Renaissance repertoire with Noah Greenberg's New York Pro Musica. He went on to sing with Leonard Bernstein and the New York Philharmonic and other major orchestras, as well as with the Monte Carlo Opera. He has performed and recorded with Yo-Yo Ma, Samuel Sanders, Placido Domingo, William Bolcom, Brian Zeger, and Graham Johnson in music ranging from Beethoven to Richard Rodgers; premiered works by composers including Menotti, Hindemith (under the composer's direction), John Corigliano, Lowell Liebermann, Milton Babbitt, Ned Rorem, and Lukas Foss; and hosted his own BBC series with orchestra.

White has sung for six American presidents—Truman, Kennedy, Carter, Ford, Reagan, and Clinton—and also for Britain's Queen Mother and Prince Charles, Monaco's royal family, and Pope John Paul II.

As a youngster, White acted and sang on New York radio with stars such as Bing Crosby, Frank Sinatra, Humphrey Bogart, Beatrice Lillie, and Bob Hope. His recent CDs include Hyperion's *Bird Songs at Eventide*, with pianist Stephen Hough; Irving Berlin songs and duets on *Berlin Lieder*, with Marilyn Horne and pianist Dick Hyman; and *Songs of Lowell Liebermann*, with the composer at the piano.

White received the 2007 Award for Artistic Excellence from the Lincoln Center Chamber Music Society, held the William Schuman Scholars Chair for 2008 at the Juilliard School of Music, and is a member of the Directors Council of the New York City Opera. He serves on the CUNY graduate voice faculty and has been a member of the Juilliard voice faculty since 1992.

Interview

By Permission of Robert White

RW   I first met Sam Barber in 1961. Gian Carlo Menotti had written a part for me in his opera *The Labyrinth,* written for NBC television—Judith Raskin and John Reardon sang in it[1]—and he had invited me with a lot of the other singers to try out this opera. We went to Mt. Kisco, where he had a beautiful home in the country. That's where I met Sam.

AJ   Were you associated closely with him?

RW   Yes, I certainly was. Sam became a very good friend, not only to me but also to my family. He knew my brothers and sisters, the whole crew. When I had my first student digs in Manhattan, Sam was there at the house-warming with a lot of other musical friends. I last saw him on January 11, 1981, in the hospital, where a very touching and astonishing thing took place. Ransom Wilson, the flutist, had gathered some of the kids from Juilliard—my old alma mater—to play and visit with Sam at the hospital.[2] We all knew how desperately ill he was and that the time wasn't all that long. About thirty people came and crowded into a small room on the floor where Sam was. John Browning was there, William Schuman and his wife, Alice Tully,[3] and John Corigliano. Many of our lives, especially through Spoleto, had been enriched by Gian Carlo and Sam.

Ransom Wilson had said, "Let us go to Sam's bedside and make some music for him while he is still with us." He was ill and in his wheelchair, but he knew we were there and spoke with us. I had wondered what to bring Sam, and I found a copy of a photo made about two years earlier at a party after a concert given by James Galway. It shows Sam, me, Lynn Harrell, and Jimmy Galway.[4] We'd had a fantastic time at my party and looked like we were having a ball. When I walked into the room and gave him this in a little frame, he was so taken that he started to show this picture of the four of us to everyone about him.

---

1. Judith Raskin (1928–84), American lyric soprano and educator. John Reardon (1930–2009), American baritone with a career in contemporary opera.

2. Ransom Wilson (1951–), prominent American flutist and conductor, professor of flute at Yale University.

3. Alice Bigelow Tully (1902–93), American singer and patroness whose donations created Alice Tully Hall at the Lincoln Center for the Performing Arts, New York City, in 1969.

4. Lynn Harrell (1944–), American cellist with an international reputation. Sir James Galway (1939–), celebrated flutist born in Northern Ireland and known as "the Man with the Golden Flute."

The kids from Juilliard played the string quartet—the original version of
the famous *Adagio* [1936]. It was very beautiful, very moving, and done
with a lot of love. Then some wind players came and played *Summer Music*
[1955] for him. A little piano was wheeled in, and John Browning played
a Chopin ballade, I think, then Robert de Gaetano played a piece of
Sam's on this out-of-tune upright. Then Gian Carlo said, "Bob, why don't
you sing something for us?" I didn't want to do a cappella but I wanted
something to cheer up the occasion, so the first thing I thought of was
"Smilin' Through" instead of something classical.[5] Sam's aunt was Louise
Homer, the famous contralto, and she was friends with Alma Gluck and
John McCormack, who sang ballads too.[6] People responded to "Smilin'
Through," and then I wanted something bouncy so I sang "Trottin' to
the Fair."[7] Sam took my hand, moving it to the jaunting rhythm.

His first cousin was there, the daughter of Louise Homer. It thrilled me
to meet the direct descendant and I said, "I'm going to London, and
among other things I'm going to record 'Whispering Hope'[8]—the duet
Louise Homer and Alma Gluck did in 1915." And she said, "Mr. White,
my mother said that song was the foundation of our family's good luck!"

AJ   I gather he was a very shy man.

RW   He was—and a true gentleman. I never met anyone with quite the wonderful qualities of a kind of shyness and an ironic sense of humor. He was
very urbane and very kind. He did a lot of nice things for a lot of people,
giving advice to composers and performers.

AJ   What kind of humor did he have?

RW   I used to love to go around New York City on my bicycle, a ten-speed Italian racer. I lived over on the West Side and Sam lived on the very posh
East Side. One beautiful early summer day I was riding along on the bike

---

5. "Smilin' Through" (1919), popular ballad with lyrics and music by Arthur A. Penn.
It was incorporated into the eponymous Broadway musical, used in films, widely performed and recorded, and remained popular for decades.

6. Alma Gluck (1884–1938), American soprano from a Romanian-Jewish immigrant
family who moved from opera to great success with popular ballads. Her second husband
was Efrem Zimbalist, who later married Mary Louise Curtis Bok, founder of the Curtis
Institute. John McCormack (1884–1945), enormously successful Irish-born tenor.

7. "Trottin' to the Fair," from *Songs of Erin, 50 Irish Folksongs*, op. 76 (1901). Irish ballad
by Alfred Perceval Graves set by Sir Charles Villiers Stanford (1852–1924).

8. "Whispering Hope" (1868), popular song by Septimus Winner (1827–1902), American composer, teacher, and publisher based in Philadelphia.

and I saw Sam. I stopped and said, "Sam, how are you?" He was looking so elegant in a really fine suede jacket and buck shoes and he said, "Well, what are *you* doing on this side of town?"

Another time I was walking up Fifth Avenue in the business district, and I was behind him. In the crowds of shoppers passing I started to whistle the theme of the quintet from the end of *Vanessa* [1958]. [*whistles*] All of a sudden Sam stopped, turned around, and I said, "Did that surprise you?" He said, "Well, I'm glad that *somebody* knows my music in this city!" [*laughs*]

AJ   What was he like dealing with musicians on musical matters?

RW   Again, I would say he was very kind. He would give help and criticism. He was very articulate, going right to the heart of the matter if he didn't like something—and he would say why. I never heard Sam put down other young composers whose music might be in a totally different vein from his own lyrical expression. And I always felt that Samuel Barber, for the American way of thinking and music making, had many of the attributes and qualities and certainly the high aims of Benjamin Britten. I'm not equating the two composers; I'm just saying that Sam was toiling in that same vineyard in a sense: his whole life was one aimed at quality.

AJ   He was a performer himself, of course—a singer.

RW   Another thing that made us feel close was the fact that Sam was a singer. He had a beautiful baritone voice. I think he was the only student in the history of the Curtis Institute who was a triple major—in piano, voice, and composition.

AJ   Did you hear him sing?

RW   Yes, he used to accompany me in classical pieces, and he would sing at the same time. I remember his singing "Sure on This Shining Night" [1938], one of his most beautiful songs.

AJ   And he recorded *Dover Beach* [1931].

RW   He did, and he was very proud of the fact that it sounded so good! [*laughs*]

AJ   Have you any thoughts on his writing for the voice?

RW   It was very lyrical. When you listen to *Vanessa* there's so much glorious stuff for the voice in there, and it's so full of great beauty, great feeling, and great intensity.

AJ   *Vanessa* was successful to a certain extent; *Antony and Cleopatra* [1966] was, to put it mildly, much less so.

RW   Yes, well, that's history, and it's a known fact that Sam was very shattered by the response to *Antony and Cleopatra*. I was there through a lot of the gestation period of that opera. One summer up at the house Sam said he couldn't get a kid to sing as the sword bearer for Antony in a crucial scene. He had to look good onstage and sing a plaintive melody: "Oh, Antony." Antony is so lovesick, wants to commit suicide and can't do it, so he asks the sword bearer to kill him. He agrees but takes the knife and kills himself instead. It's an important moment in the opera. Sam said that Franco Zeffirelli had auditioned dozens of kids, and they didn't come up to it. I thought of a kid I knew in the choir of an Episcopal church in New York I used to sing in, Bruce Scott. He got the job. Sam said he was eternally grateful because many of the critiques of the opera said the boy got across both the feeling and his words.

AJ   Why do you think the opera was such a failure?

RW   I was at the opening, and I think it was overblown. Much has been said and written that there was the problem of Zeffirelli's directing. I can't really, in a qualified way, go into all of that. The whole thing was overwhelming: the opening of this brand-new house and what that represented. But in 1975—for the first time I think since the fiasco at the Met—the Juilliard School put on *Antony and Cleopatra* in a performance beautifully done. Sam had made changes, and it was such a vindication. It got tremendous reviews. When the opera wasn't aggrandized, it had so much going for it. We were all quite astonished and happy for Sam.

AJ   So the production rather than the conception of the opera was at fault?

RW   I would say it was the production and the auspices under which it took place. Sam needed something leaner. He went back to the workshop for the Juilliard production, and sure enough, out came a thing of great beauty—I remember being very moved by the performance.

AJ   In the UK the reputation of Samuel Barber as a composer is high in some quarters, less so in others. How is he rated as a serious composer in America?

RW   Very high. Samuel Barber has for years been considered one of America's great classical composers. It has nothing to do with the personal friendship I had with him: I think as the years go on, Sam's tremendous stature will become more and more evident. I was in on the composing of the Piano Concerto [1962], which I remember very well—a beautiful piece. And the Piano Sonata [1949] is a masterpiece, with that fugal ending.

AJ   Does his romanticism put some people off?

RW   Who really sounds like Barber? Let's get down to brass tacks with this. To me, Barber sounds like Barber—an idiom of lyricism and musicality—and Beethoven sounds like Beethoven. I don't care what bag any given composer is in, it's how well they do what they are doing that separates the wheat from the chaff.

AJ   Why do you think he wrote so little in the last twenty years of his life?

RW   Sam was born into a very comfortable family. I guess you would call it a very posh upbringing by any standards, American or otherwise, and a very educated family. He liked the good life, and he was a very elegant man. But I think he was weary from the reception of *Antony and Cleopatra;* that put him into a very unfruitful period. Before that he was always busy. I remember him writing *Andromache's Farewell* [1962] for soprano and orchestra. John Corigliano and I suggested he use Martina Arroyo. But everything was very active up until that opera and its opening at the Met. That disheartened Sam tremendously—he pulled back. Also, he moved into a very beautiful apartment on Fifth Avenue; that was a big change in his life, and it took up a lot of his energies and time.

AJ   Did he ever resent the popularity of the *Adagio for Strings* to the exclusion of most of his other works?

RW   I can honestly tell you yes. From his own lips I heard him say it to me more than once. And I could never quite understand it. I even argued with him, saying: "Sam, no matter what you say, the thing is so outrageously beautiful. Just think if you had never written it!" [*laughs*] But it's the old thing: everyone who met him and didn't really know anything else about him would jump on the bandwagon of the *Adagio,* so in a sense he got tired of hearing about it. But I'm sure in his heart of hearts the same thing that caused him to write it had to lurk there. When I heard it in the original version while Sam sat there in the hospital, all those thoughts were going through my head.

I remember a particularly happy day spent in his company when the great ships arrived in New York Harbor in 1976. There were hundreds of tall-mast nineteenth-century ships to celebrate the two hundredth anniversary of America. My brother Philip was a member of the club at the top of the World Trade Center—the restaurant was called Windows on the World[9]—and we invited Sam. So we sat together on the 107th floor overlooking the Statue of Liberty, looking at the ships and drinking champagne. When we had spent the day together Sam said, "This, to me, is like the America of my childhood: we all felt so proud of Old Glory!" Here was Sam, so urbane and—to a New Yorker—very European. He was just like a kid that day. No mention of music. We were just a bunch of Americans having a hell of a good time on our two hundredth birthday. He was glad to be down-home American again.

---

5. All this was destroyed on September 11, 2001.

Part Six

Publishers and Critics

Chapter Fourteen

H. Wiley Hitchcock

Interview with Peter Dickinson, 1192 Park Avenue, New York City, May 10, 1981

Introduction

H. Wiley Hitchcock (1923–2007) was a pioneer in the field of American music studies. His *Music in the United States: A Historical Introduction* (1969) was widely influential and has gone through four editions. It broke new ground by considering all kinds of American music, both serious and popular, for which he invented the terms "cultivated" and "vernacular." Hitchcock's name will always be associated with Charles Ives—he and Vivian Perlis were responsible for the comprehensive Charles Ives Centennial Festival Conference held in New York and New Haven in 1974. *An Ives Celebration* was the book that arose from the conference; it came out in 1977, the year Hitchcock also published a short monograph on Ives. One of his last projects was a massively documented edition of *129 Songs* by Ives in the American Musicological Society's series MUSA—Music of the USA (2004). But, like other American musicologists of his generation, Hitchcock first worked on European music: his expertise on seventeenth-century French composers, notably François Couperin, was recognized by his appointment in 1995 as Chevalier of the Ordre des Arts et des Lettres.

Hitchcock was born near Detroit, Michigan, and earned his BA at Dartmouth College—where the piano became his instrument—and his master's at the University of Michigan. He spent a decade teaching at Michigan; another at Hunter College, New York; and in 1971 became founder-director of the Institute for Studies in American Music at Brooklyn College, City University of New York (CUNY). He was co-editor with Stanley Sadie of the four-volume *New Grove Dictionary of American Music* (1986).

In 1990, *A Celebration of American Music: Words and Music in Honor of H. Wiley Hitchcock* was published—a five-hundred-page tribute drawing on leading American scholars and composers. Hitchcock was named Distinguished Professor at CUNY in 1980 and retired in 1993. He was president of the Charles Ives Society, president of the American Musicological Society (1990–92), and editor of several important series on American music. One of his last completed projects was an edition of the first of the two operas Virgil Thomson wrote with Gertrude Stein: *Four Saints in Three Acts.*

Interview

By Permission of Janet Hitchcock

PD   Many of us who have been involved with American music have formed the habit of looking for American qualities such as those found in Copland, Gershwin, and popular music. As a result, do you think some other composers such as MacDowell or Barber, who do not have those obvious characteristics, tend to get a raw deal?

HWH Yes, I do. I think it's a very limiting kind of view, and I don't think it's necessary. For example, this morning I heard a program of music by Michael Tippett.[1] It never occurred to me to think: "Now, let's see, how English is this? What aspects of English background do I hear?"

PD   And yet, you can hear his English background. Are you not aware of that?

HWH No. I simply don't know his music that well. Now that I think of it, I might draw some parallels between that experience of hearing Tippett simply as music and one's hearing Barber simply as music.

PD   Regardless of American connections.

HWH Yes indeed.

PD   And yet, in your book you pick out the very American *Knoxville* as an example of Barber's particular gifts.[2] Do you think that from a historical point of view Barber's impact will be more through his songs than the larger works?

HWH Well, I am certainly not among the admirers of the operas, even *Vanessa*.[3] I prefer the smaller pieces. The Piano Sonata I consider uneven and dangerously flawed, as opposed to, let's say, the *Capricorn Concerto*, which is slighter.[4] *Knoxville* for me is very special because of the exquisite

---

1. Sir Michael Tippett (1905–98).

2. H. Wiley Hitchcock, with Kyle Gann, *Music in the United States: A Historical Introduction* (Upper Saddle River, NJ: Prentice-Hall, 1969, 1974, 1988, 2000). *Knoxville: Summer of 1915,* op. 24 (1948), for soprano and orchestra.

3. *Vanessa,* op. 32 (libretto by Menotti), opera premiered at the Metropolitan in New York City on January 15, 1958.

4. Piano Sonata, op. 26 (1949); *Capricorn Concerto,* op. 21 (1944).

text of James Agee and the perfect marriage, it seems to me, of the nostalgic quality of that text and Barber's music.

PD   Could I take you back to *Vanessa*, because if one is looking for some achievement in American opera, then *Vanessa*, we've been told by Menotti, was planned as a libretto to provide opportunities for exactly what Barber wanted to do as a composer. Do you think Barber failed, or is it something to do with opera at this stage?

HWH   I saw a production of *Vanessa* many years ago, not recently. I recall my reaction was that the libretto was slightly uncomfortable for Barber, that it was more a Menotti work than a Barber work, if I can put it that way. I felt even more strongly about [the unsuitability of the libretto for] *Antony and Cleopatra*.

PD   What sort of flaws are you thinking of in the Piano Sonata?

HWH   I think a kind of unevenness of inspiration or level of compositional skill, a kind of contrived quality to each of the movements that attempt something in fact not quite achieved.

PD   We've been talking about American qualities. The syncopated final fugue of the Piano Sonata has almost the breathless pace of the Elliott Carter example.[5] This could be American?

HWH   Conceivably. I don't know whether you know Theodore Chanler's *The Second Joyful Mystery*?[6] It's also a fugue remarkably similar in the rhythmic quality you adduced in the Barber. I've often wondered if he knew that piece.

PD   From a historical point of view, how would you place Barber in terms of his colleagues and contemporaries? I notice in your book you spend more time on William Schuman. Is that because you feel Schuman is more important in the long run?

HWH   I think Barber has been a very lucky composer. I mean, for such a small oeuvre as Barber turned out, to have had the performances and the level of production he had, I think he has been very lucky. He has been a very careful composer, and I think he hasn't taken the chances Schuman and others have. Schuman has been willing to risk more failures.

---

5. Elliott Carter (1908–), Piano Sonata (1945–46).

6. Theodore Chanler (1902–61). *The Second Joyful Mystery* (ca. 1948) is for soprano, alto, and two pianos.

PD   Without ever achieving the large public, which is such a feature of Barber's *Adagio,* for example. Do you sneer at the *Adagio?*

HWH   I do not sneer at it at all. I think it's a marvelous piece—a spectacular success as a piece of music. I still think it's a very careful piece but one that reflects Barber as a gifted composer who really knows his craft.

PD   As a musicologist you understand the situation in previous centuries, but in the twentieth century we seem to have penalized composers who aren't groundbreakers. Those composers who retain a public and who communicate seem to have been at a disadvantage with the profession but not with their audiences. Are we applying a double standard from a historical point of view?

HWH   Oh, sure! [*laughs*] Historians love to see the people who are taking the chances on the leading edge. They're more interesting than those who are manifestly successful from the beginning with audiences, like Barber or Morton Gould.[7]

PD   Is it because a piece by Barber makes an impact at a first hearing?

HWH   That's been true of a number of pieces—the first two *Essays for Orchestra,* the *Adagio,* and *Vanessa* as a repertory success.[8]

AJ[9]   It's been said that only Americans can understand *Knoxville.*

HWH   The text itself has imagery that is very familiar to a lot of Americans in middle age today. That is going back to a slightly more innocent America and days of rocking chairs on front porches, hearing the ice cream man come along, and hearing the trolley screaming on its rails. For people of my age—I'm in my mid-fifties—these are images that evoke very positive memories, and Barber catches that feeling of recollection through a kind of gauzy cloud of sweet memory without becoming saccharine. It's on the edge.

PD   It's comparable to some of the Ives pieces about childhood, like his song "The Greatest Man"?

HWH   Very interesting point—there is that element of nostalgia and memory.

PD   And that reverting to childhood is quite an American thing. It emerges in literature too—Tom Sawyer, for example.[10]

---

7. Morton Gould (1913–96), prolific composer, conductor, pianist, and entrepreneur.
8. *Essay for Orchestra,* op. 12 (1937); *Second Essay for Orchestra,* op. 19 (1942).
9. Arthur Johnson, BBC producer.
10. *The Adventures of Tom Sawyer* (1876) by Mark Twain (1835–1920).

HWH Indeed, not to mention *The Deerslayer* [*laughs*] and others evoking an image of the past.[11]

PD If Ives looks back to times that can never be reached again—his childhood, his father, and the Civil War—then is there that pattern in Barber too?

HWH It's pretty dangerous to generalize because for every *Knoxville: Summer of 1915* in Barber's output there is *A Hand of Bridge;* for every *Souvenirs* there is an *Excursions,* which is not necessarily nostalgic.[12]

PD It seems to me that the model for *Excursions* is not quite accurately observed and that the distance from the style—the kind of parody at which Stravinsky excelled—isn't quite right either.

HWH I completely agree. The model is misheard and the result not felt deeply. There is no parody, it seems to me, in the sense of an amused sidelong glance at something.[13]

PD *Souvenirs,* sometimes compared to Walton's *Façade,* doesn't quite add up?[14] Is it that he's not a big enough personality to take popular idioms and command them, or is it a certain instability?

HWH I think it's a certain lack of sympathy with them. With *Souvenirs,* Barber said he imagined it being choreographed, the scene being the Palm Court of the Plaza Hotel. He goes on, but the very words he chooses slightly suggest he's looking down his nose a little bit at the pop music of the turn of the century.[15]

PD He doesn't have Poulenc's easy relationship with popular idioms, yet Barber was a great admirer of Poulenc—Menotti said so—and I think his songs show this. The *Hermit Songs* show him to be a very polished song composer.[16]

---

11. *The Deerslayer* (1841) by James Fennimore Cooper (1779–1851).

12. *A Hand of Bridge,* op. 35 (1959), mini-opera lasting nine minutes with a vocal score cover design by Andy Warhol; *Souvenirs,* op. 28 (1952), piano duet (also solo and two pianos) and ballet; *Four Excursions,* op. 20 (1942–44), piano solo.

13. Barber said he wrote *Four Excursions* just to prove he could write "American music." Barbara B. Heyman, *Samuel Barber: The Composer and His Music* (New York: Oxford University Press, 1992), 232.

14. William Walton (1902–83); *Façade* (1922–29), spoken poems by Edith Sitwell with chamber ensemble.

15. Barber actually said: "One might imagine a divertissement in a setting of the Palm Court at the Plaza Hotel, the year about 1914, epoch of the first tangos; 'Souvenirs'—remembered with affection, not in irony or with tongue in check, but in amused tenderness." Heyman, *Samuel Barber: The Composer and His Music,* 328–29.

16. *Hermit Songs,* op. 29 (1952–53).

AJ How high do the *Hermit Songs* rate in the American repertoire?

HWH Very high indeed. I suppose if one were to cite the important body of songs by American composers of the twentieth century, one would say Ives, Barber of the *Hermit Songs,* Theodore Chanler of the *Epitaphs,* and Ned Rorem. Virgil Thomson perhaps.

PD Copland's Emily Dickinson songs?[17]

HWH Many people consider them [comparable].

AJ How much of Barber's distance from popular idioms could be related to his coming from a rich family?

HWH I don't know that much about Barber's personal life, but I would guess it was more related to his musical background and conservatory training from a very early age. He was a member of a family with musical pretensions in the world of serious concert music. I would relate it to those two things rather than to wealth per se.

PD Initially, Barber did need to influence people to support him and his music and managed it very successfully.

HWH I don't think there was a lot of money there, although he came from a rather patrician background.

PD You could say that just as his music wooed listeners, he managed to woo his patrons?

HWH I never met him, but my impression was that he was indeed a charming person.

---

17. *Twelve Poems of Emily Dickinson* (1950).

Chapter Fifteen

Hans W. Heinsheimer

Interview with Peter Dickinson, New York City, May 13, 1981

Introduction

Hans W. Heinsheimer (1900–1993) was born in Karlsruhe, Germany, and came to the United States in 1938, where he consolidated his reputation as one of the most influential music publishers of the twentieth century. He studied law but gave it up in 1923 to work in music publishing for Universal Edition in Vienna. There he introduced Alban Berg to Louis Krasner, thus paving the way for Berg's Violin Concerto. When Heinsheimer was working for Boosey and Hawkes in New York, he generously found an ingenious way of supporting the destitute Béla Bartók in his final years in the city. Heinsheimer wrote three books of memoirs—*Menagerie in F Sharp* (1947), *Fanfare for Two Pigeons* (1952), and *Best Regards to Aida* (1968)—and also wrote reviews for Austrian newspapers and radio stations and American journals.[1]

Interview

By Permission of the Estate of Hans W. Heinsheimer

HH   I came to Schirmer's in 1947 from Boosey and Hawkes, where I spent ten years as the publisher of Aaron Copland and Béla Bartók. Then I came to Schirmer's and started my association with Samuel Barber as the most important composer in the Schirmer catalog at that time—Bernstein wasn't there yet—and I was in charge of promoting Barber's music. I

---

1. "Obituary: Hans W. Heinsheimer Dies at 93: Top Publisher of Classical Music," *The New York Times*, October 14, 1993.

was connected with the premiere of *Vanessa* and later on with *Antony and Cleopatra.*

Now, the interesting thing from my point of view is that *Antony and Cleopatra* was an absolute turning point in the life of Barber. It was a terrible catastrophe from which he never recovered. I wrote an article about Barber in a magazine here after his death.[2] A friend who was a psychologist always established a link between cancer and psychic life. I cannot prove it—I am not a doctor—but I think his sickness started at this time. The interesting thing is that Barber's life took a complete turn from that moment: he never wrote anything of importance after that. This was in 1966, fifteen years before his death.

Later he wrote a song cycle called *Despite and Still* [1968]—a defiant title meaning that, despite this disaster, he would still compose.[3] It meant also "despite" all the criticism leveled at his style of music. People began to wonder, "Can you really continue composing like that in the day and age of Berio, Stockhausen, and everybody else?"[4] And he was absolutely conscious of that; he knew that was a problem. It's interesting that Dietrich Fischer-Dieskau asked him to do a song cycle for him, hoping he would get another *Winterreise*, I guess.[5] And suddenly Sam said, "I can't find any lyrics." Now, he had always found lyrics, but he finally came up with two or three little songs and Fischer-Dieskau was terribly disappointed. He had a commission from the Pittsburgh Symphony Orchestra; he wrote a piece called *Fadograph* that was really very disappointing.[6] There was an oratorio with a text by Neruda, *The Lovers,* which did not get anywhere— disappeared after one or two performances—and later on the *Third Essay for Orchestra* that had a few performances.[7] In other words, the great Barber who wrote the concertos, not to mention the *Adagio for Strings, Vanessa,* the beautiful *Knoxville* . . . it was all gone.

PD   What was Barber like to deal with as a composer? Did he revise a lot? Was he very meticulous?

---

2. Hans W. Heinsheimer, "Adagio for Sam," *Opera News* (March 14, 1981): 30–32.

3. The symbolism of the title is acute, but see Barbara B. Heyman, *Samuel Barber: The Composer and His Music* (New York: Oxford University Press, 1992), 472.

4. Luciano Berio (1925–2003), Italian composer. Karlheinz Stockhausen (1928–2007), German composer. Both became prominent on the international new music scene following World War II and remained influential.

5. *Three Songs,* op. 45 (1972). Dietrich Fischer-Dieskau (1925–).

6. *Fadograph of a Yestern Scene,* op. 44 (1971), Pittsburgh Symphony Orchestra/Steinberg, September 11, 1971, Heinz Hall, Pittsburgh.

7. *The Lovers,* op. 43, for baritone and orchestra (1971); *Third Essay for Orchestra,* op. 47, for orchestra (1978). Pablo Neruda (1904–73), Chilean writer and diplomat.

HH He was very meticulous, but he did not revise much at all.[8] He was always absolutely reliable. The Piano Concerto was one of the few occasions when he didn't finish in time. He had trouble with the third movement, and John Browning had to learn it about ten days before the first performance.

He was very careful with his manuscripts from the beginning, and that was it. Usually they would be engraved, published, and performed just as they were written. The famous exception was the Second Symphony, which he wrote while he was in the army. This is an amusing story. He came to me one day in my office at Schirmer's, and we had lunch—the champagne cocktail he always wanted—and I asked him, "How is it that all your music is successful except the Second Symphony?" He said: "It's very simple: it's no good. And I tell you something, let's go right up in the warehouse and destroy it!" He said, "Now we go." We went to the rental library, and he took out the beautiful written sheets and tore them up. A porter was called with a barrow—and that was the end of the Second Symphony.[9]

It's interesting that he wrote only one of everything. One symphony was very good—the second was no good; one opera—the second was no good; one piano concerto, one cello concerto, and so forth. Only the songs, of course—that's different. There he was a master and wrote forty or fifty songs. [Actually one hundred and thirty, some published since this interview.]

PD Composers aren't always right about their own music. Why did you let him destroy the outer movements of the Second Symphony?

HH He was such a serious man; I was sure he was right. And also the fact that it was never performed; there must have been a reason. It was published. Every conductor had the pocket score and could have done it. I had no reason to doubt his judgment.

PD Why did he think it was no good just because it wasn't performed? Look at all the pieces by Ives . . .

---

8. According to Barbara Heyman, this is contradicted by revisions and drafts at the Library of Congress. See Heyman, *A Comprehensive Catalog of the Complete Works of Samuel Barber*, forthcoming.

9. Second Symphony (dedicated to the Army Air Forces), op. 19 (1944), premiered by the Boston Symphony Orchestra under Koussevitsky on March 3, 1944. The second movement of this symphony, under the title *Night Flight*, was salvaged and performed separately. Barber later used material from the first movement for *Antony and Cleopatra* and *Fadograph of a Yestern Scene*. In 1984 a set of parts was discovered by Andrew Schenk that enabled the symphony to be reinstated and recorded by him with the New Zealand Symphony Orchestra on Stradivari SCD8012 (1989).

HH   Because he wrote it under duress. It was in honor of the air force, so to speak. He was carried from one base to another to study army life and talk to people and reflect this somehow. It was all no good. He just hated it, and that was it.

PD   As a publisher who's been in touch with the taste of the public, can you say what it is that appeals in Barber's music?

HH   Well, he is really one of the very few composers in this age who writes in this romantic, pleasant style. The songs, of course, are as beautiful as any songs can be. In songs particularly you cannot write really modern music. Britten wrote beautiful songs. You cannot write songs in the style of really contemporary music—you can write them, but they will not be sung! His music, in the old-fashioned sense, is excellent. It doesn't establish any school; he had no students, or almost none; there is no Barber following.

PD   Did you see very much influence of Menotti on Barber?

HH   I would think if anything it's the other way around. Barber was a much more important composer. Menotti used to have great success as a stage writer, but no musician would take him seriously. To assume that this would have any influence on a great composer like Barber is not for real.

PD   You're saying "great composer?"

HH   *Knoxville* is a typical example—an absolutely beautiful work—the songs, the Piano Concerto, the Cello Concerto. He is an important composer in his own style. Unfortunately, his career ended fifteen years before his death.

PD   It's been said he was the most commercially successful American serious composer . . .

HH   After Copland. Then Barber too. It was certainly enough to maintain a very comfortable living.

PD   Why did the *Adagio for Strings* become the popular classic of its time?

HH   Well, first, it's short. It's easier for a piece to become a folk pop and a classic when it's nine minutes than when it's thirty-five minutes. It can be put in any program; it's easy to perform, it plays itself. Toscanini introduced it, which gave it immediately a sendoff of importance. It's a very practical piece, and practicability—I've been in the publishing business for fifty years—is half the battle.

PD   Do you remember why the vocal version of that piece was made to the text of the *Agnus Dei?*

HH   Somebody requested it and he rewarded them, but it never became really successful or popular.[10]

PD   He was very fortunate in his connections with performers, wasn't he?

HH   Absolutely. It is amazing when you look at this beginning of a young composer. He started out with Molinari in Italy, Bruno Walter, Toscanini, Leontyne Price.[11] He always got the best performances—Eleanor Steber commissioned *Knoxville,* and so on. Horowitz gave the first performance of the Piano Sonata in Schirmer's at that time in a building on 43rd Street.[12] The director's room was on the seventh floor. Eighty people were invited. It was very difficult to get the piano up there because it didn't go in the elevator. They had to put it on the roof of the elevator, and it was terribly dangerous: people were in danger of being crushed. Horowitz played it twice, and there was a nice party. He said he wanted everybody in the building to be invited. They all came, got drinks and sandwiches and a handshake from Horowitz and Barber.

PD   He's talked about as witty and amusing—do you remember any examples?

HH   He was witty, but he was mostly rather morose, irritable, in a difficult mood when he felt things were not going right. I can't recall him as a particularly easygoing or humorous man.

PD   Things not going right—for him of all people?

HH   Yes, but he wanted more and more—not materialistic but in success, recognition, performances. He could easily be sarcastic about other musicians and performers. The wit he had was sometimes at the expense of others.

PD   Did you find that Barber's reputation rose steadily?

HH   Yes, because he added new things. In Barber's case the old things did not drop down. He started with the *Adagio for Strings,* the early songs, and the First Symphony, and they kept going so his repertoire always increased until about 1966. The ASCAP figures show no decrease at all.

---

10. This is no longer true, with thirty-five recordings in 2008; *Agnus Dei* (1967).

11. Bernardino Molinari (1880–1952), Italian conductor who gave the premiere of the First Symphony in Rome in 1936; Bruno Walter (1876–1972), German-born conductor who took French and then American citizenship, gave the premiere of the *Second Essay for Orchestra* with the New York Philharmonic Symphony Orchestra on April 16–19, 1942; Arturo Toscanini (1867–1957) presented both the *Adagio for Strings* and the *First Essay for Orchestra* in 1938.

12. January 4, 1950.

PD   Several people have mentioned that there seems to have been a crisis with the selling of the house and the break with Menotti?

HH   It's difficult to overestimate the absolute disaster of the Metropolitan. He physically disappeared after that, and for several days we didn't know where he was. And then he called me, saying: "I'm at the pier [on 57th Street] and I'm taking a boat to Europe." He really fled. Weeks passed before we heard from him from Europe. This was a terrible shock.[13]

PD   Especially with a composer used to such continuous success?

HH   Of course.

PD   People have said he was very lucky, with the right kind of family background.

HH   I think you can say that from the beginning. Then suddenly this happens. It was such a prominent failure—the opening of the Metropolitan! You couldn't ask for greater exposure. It was a really awful night. We all sat there realizing this is going down the drain.

PD   Any final memories?

HH   When the *Toccata Festiva* for organ and orchestra was performed in Philadelphia, Mary Curtis Bok Zimbalist said she was concerned at not having given Barber a large enough commission fee. So she said, "I have a feeling that Mt. Kisco needs another wing; feel free to build it." So they did. That's the type of Maecenas she was![14]

PD   He had an ability to find generous friends.

HH   Barber was the only one of all the composers I worked with who would give me a lovely present. For example, these are dictionaries in all languages—from Barber. In my country home I have beautiful Italian mugs he and Menotti gave me. He was attentive and nice, friendly with my wife, who was a dentist. He was not her patient, but he consulted her

---

13. Barber may have planned a vacation in Italy anyway. See Heyman, *Samuel Barber: The Composer and His Music*, 451.

14. *Toccata Festiva*, op. 36 (1960). According to Heyman, Barber's fee was two thousand dollars, but he waived it because of the support Mary Curtis Bok had given him over the years. Her support for extending the house could have reflected this; she had already paid for the new organ as well. Heinsheimer also said: "It was a terrible thing that they gave up Mt. Kisco because he moved into an apartment on 5th Avenue and he never felt at home there. It was not the atmosphere he needed to write."

about trouble with his teeth and loved to discuss it with her and tease her about it. We visited Mt. Kisco any number of times. I did a big story on *Antony and Cleopatra* for the *Saturday Review,* and when I took it to Mt. Kisco he wasn't there.[15] So I walked in—the doors were always open—put it on his desk with a little note, and left. He called me later. It was pleasant to work with him. He was a fine gentleman, terribly well-educated, and the number of important people around him was enormous.

---

15. Hans W. Heinsheimer, "Birth of an Opera," *Saturday Review* (September 17, 1966): 49–50, 56–58.

Chapter Sixteen

Edward P. Murphy

Interview with Peter Dickinson, New York City, May 12, 1981

Introduction

Edward P. Murphy (1939–) is the former president and chief executive officer of the National Music Publishers Association, Inc., representing more than nine hundred American music publishers and the global protection of their music copyrights. He joined NMPA as executive vice president in 1983, was elected president of the Harry Fox Agency—its licensing subsidiary representing more than twenty-seven thousand music publishers—the following year, and became president and chief executive officer of NMPA and the Harry Fox Agency in 1985. Previously, he served as president of G. Schirmer, Inc., the firm with which he was associated for most of his working life.

Murphy serves on the board of the Songwriters Hall of Fame, the National Music Council, and the New York University masters program in music business and technology; he also runs Harmony Media LLC. Murphy has represented his profession on the ASCAP[1] board, the Music Publishers Association, the International Federation of Popular Music Publishers, and the Bureau international des sociétés gérant les droits d'enregistrement et de reproduction mécanique. He founded the International Copyright Commission and has been regularly called upon by the U.S. Copyright Office and other government entities to provide guidance on music industry and copyright issues.

A few of Murphy's many honors include the President's Award, given by the Songwriters Guild of America (1999); the Indie Award (2001) from the New York chapter of the Association of Independent Music Publishers; and the Abe Olman Publisher Award (2002) from the Songwriters Hall of Fame.

---

1. American Society of Composers, Authors and Publishers, established in 1914.

Interview

By Permission of Edward P. Murphy

EM   I first met Sam in 1975. We would meet for lunch once every month or two and discuss his music, the industry, new composers and new music, and what he thought of current activities. I found him to be humorous and meticulous about things, demanding in many ways. His music reflects that attitude—he was a real professional. In dealing with him, one had to be as much of a professional as he was.

I think John Corigliano was the only composer Sam brought to our house—he had great respect for his work.[2] Sam was a member of ASCAP and interested in activities involving serious music.

Sam was with Schirmer's from the very beginning of his career.[3] We published his first work. Another aspect of Sam's personality was his extreme loyalty to our house, and we were loyal to him.

PD   How did he feel, in a rather hostile professional environment, with the avant-garde getting all the publicity? How did he see himself?

EM   I don't think he felt particularly intimidated; Sam always did what he wanted to do. His music reflected his own attitudes, and he was going to continue to compose what he believed he should. What other people did was really of no great concern to him, and whether he was going to get public acclaim was not uppermost in his mind.

PD   But he did get acclaim in an exceptional way.

EM   Yes, he did. My impression is that he wrote what he wanted to write, and it was not for public acclaim at all. He was always happy about his notoriety for the *Adagio for Strings,* but he felt it would be nice for them to listen to all the other things he had done as well and not to be categorized

PD   How popular has it actually been? Did he not mind?

EM   He was quite pleased. It has been a smash hit and has been played in just about every country. He was flattered that Toscanini introduced it, but he didn't want to be labeled with the *Adagio*—a wish many composers share when they have certain works that have caught the public's fancy.

PD   Do you know why he made the arrangement for voices?

---

2. John Corigliano (1938–); see foreword.
3. G. Schirmer, Inc., publishing house established in New York in 1866.

EM   No. There were many different arrangements made. When it came to arrangements, we would all sit down and he would look for suggestions. He was very open about this. Our editorial staff would go over with Sam the various ways different things could be presented—he enjoyed doing this quite a bit.

PD   You say he was interested in professional matters. What was he like as a committee man?

EM   Well, through ASCAP he was intensely interested in the general activities, where we were going and making sure all the necessary credits were given properly to composers, not just himself. He was very interested in the inner workings of the society, to understand how it functioned, and he made many contributions.

PD   What has been the rise and fall in the popularity of his music over a long period?

EM   I think what you find is a little surprising. Sam's music continually grows; there hasn't been a graph where it would rise and fall—there hasn't been a fall! [*laughs*] It has been a very steady growth, not just domestically but around the world and particularly in recordings. The Soviets were interested in his music and have licensed several of his compositions. He's been performed in Poland and, of course, the UK. And it continues to climb; I haven't seen any dip at all.

PD   What was he like as a person?

EM   Sam had a very probing mind. He would often ask you a question, and you'd fully realize he knew the answer. It was really to get your reaction, but it was never done in a malicious way; it was always done to provoke thought in a humorous way. But he did insist on professionalism, even in his own lifestyle. He was meticulous, and his music does reflect that. What he turned in to us as a publisher also reflected that.

    He demanded from others but far more from himself. So we find a very curious man who was very sensitive, humorous, cutting at times, but always very loyal.

PD   And capable of being wounded, I imagine. The reception of *Antony and Cleopatra* upset him?

EM   We're all vulnerable, although he never showed this to me about *Antony and Cleopatra*. I saw the Juilliard production—not the premiere—and, like many others, thought it should be done again. A beautiful work, and we did talk about that. He accepted what had happened rather well and looked forward to new things.

PD   How would you compare him with other composers you deal with at Schirmer's such as Elliott Carter and Virgil Thomson?

EM   Each composer has a different personality. Sam was somewhat shy in terms of public performances. Mr. Carter has had more visibility. It's interesting to make that kind of comparison where Sam really never did promote himself at all. Either he thought it wasn't necessary or he didn't feel it was for him to do.

PD   This reluctance to promote himself seems almost un-American?

EM   It was a reflection of his personality. He was a gentleman, and he felt he was writing for what he believed and what he liked to do, and he was very pleased that other people liked it as well. But he felt that it was up to the publishing house to carry forward the exploitation, which we certainly did, but it was not very difficult with a talent like his.

Postscript 2005

Orlando Cole

Interview with Peter Dickinson, Philadelphia, October 13, 2005

Introduction

Orlando Cole was born in Philadelphia in 1908 and celebrated his hundredth birthday in August 2008. His father was a violinist who played in the Philadelphia Orchestra. At seven he started the piano and at twelve took up percussion. When he got to West Philadelphia High School there were no vacancies for these instruments in the orchestra, so—distinctly late—he took up the cello.

His teacher at the Curtis Institute was the English cellist and influential teacher Felix Salmond (1888–1952), who was head of the cello department from 1925 to 1942. Salmond had played in the premieres of Elgar's String Quartet and Piano Quintet,[1] was soloist in the Cello Concerto conducted by the composer in 1919, and moved to the United States in 1922. He played Barber's Cello Sonata, sometimes with the composer, after Cole gave the premiere in 1932. Cole made his New York debut while still a student in 1929 and served as Salmond's assistant after he was appointed to the Curtis faculty in 1938.

Cole taught at Curtis for seventy-five years, and his pupils included many of the world's finest cellists. He was a founder-member of the Curtis Quartet, performing with them until 1980; three of the members were together for fifty years. The quartet gave a series of concerts in London to mark King George V's Silver Jubilee in 1935[2] and played for President and Mrs. Roosevelt at the White House. The group returned to Europe in 1936 and 1937 and would have gone back in 1938 but realized it was no time to travel there because of the Hitler menace. They gave the American premiere of Barber's String Quartet in 1937.

---

1. Sir Edward Elgar (1857–1934), major British composer. String Quartet, op. 83 (1918); Piano Quintet, op. 84 (1919); Cello Concerto, op. 85 (1919).

2. There were two concerts in London and a BBC broadcast. See chapter 2 and Barbara B. Heyman, *Samuel Barber: The Composer and His Music* (New York: Oxford University Press, 1992), 123.

In 1943 Cole founded the New School of Music in Philadelphia, now affiliated with Temple University. He gave master classes throughout the United States, Europe, and the Far East.

In 1986 Cole received an honorary doctorate from the Curtis Institute; in 1990 the American String Teachers Association named him Teacher of the Year; and in 2000 Curtis gave him its first-ever Alumni Award.

As a student at Curtis, Cole remembered hearing Menotti working on his first opera *Amelia Goes to the Ball,* so the overture was included in a tribute concert to Cole held at Curtis on October 19, 2005. So was Barber's Cello Concerto, performed by one of Cole's students, Daniel Lee, who commented on his period of study during the years 1995–2002: "Mr. Cole was the kindest and most understanding teacher I ever had. He had a great deal of patience and was most generous with his time and efforts to help me with my career and achievements. I am very grateful that I had the chance to work with him." Jonah Kim confirmed this: "Everything in his music, every note, serves a purpose and that is to enchant listeners and to take them to a world where there is no ugliness. And he has communicated that message to so many musicians."[3]

Interview

By Permission of Orlando Cole

OC   We played all of Barber's early chamber music—the Serenade that was originally for string quartet;[4] *Dover Beach,* of course, which we recorded first with Rose Bampton.[5] But over at RCA they felt it's really a man's poem and perhaps it ought to have a man singer, and they made a little complaint that her diction wasn't quite clear enough. Barber really didn't want to sing it but he didn't want to coach anybody else to sing it [*laughs*], so the easier way out was to sing it himself, which he did so beautifully. It's a great treasure to have that memento of him.

---

3. Cited in "October 19 Concert to Celebrate Curtis Institute Legend Orlando Cole," *The Evening Bulletin* (Philadelphia), September 16, 2005.

4. Serenade, op. 1, premiered by the Swastika String Quartet (the name was based on a Kipling connection but was changed to Curtis Quartet in 1932), with Orlando Cole as cellist, at the Curtis Institute in a program of works by Scalero's students on May 5, 1930. It was published by Schirmer in 1944 when Barber made the version for string orchestra. Heyman, *Samuel Barber: The Composer and His Music,* 67.

5. Rose Bampton (1907–2007), prominent American opera singer much admired by Toscanini, first a mezzo and then a soprano, born in Lakewood, Ohio. She moved to Philadelphia to become a student at Curtis in 1930. She sang at the Met and other opera houses from the early 1930s until 1949.

PD   Who really was the first student at Curtis in 1924?[6]

OC   [*laughs*] We came the same day, maybe. I remember we were in classes together, and when the teacher sat us alphabetically Barber and Cole came right together most of the time. So I got to know him. He was studying piano; I don't know that in the beginning he had voice;[7] he had composition with Rosario Scalero.

PD   Was Isabelle Vengerova his piano teacher then?

OC   Not in the beginning. I think it was a man named George Boyle.[8]

PD   What was Barber like at that time? Was he very confidant?

OC   It didn't seem so. He wasn't conceited at all, just very good company, made friends. At that time both he and I were still going to high school— he would take a day off.

PD   What was Scalero like?

OC   He was a very austere, old-fashioned type of Herr Professor. I only remember they had to do a lot of study of early counterpoint—Palestrina, Josquin des Pres, and so on. But that was a wonderful thing. I think it gave Barber a solid technical background that he felt comfortable with all his life.

PD   He went on studying with Scalero for nine years!

OC   Oh, sure—in those days. I studied with my teacher for ten years before we had a graduation. Jozef Hofmann, who was director, said he didn't see the need for graduations.[9] He wanted his graduates to be judged by the way they played and not by a piece of paper. But, of course, everybody wanted that piece of paper [*laughs*], so in 1934 we had the first commencement. There's a picture of the class with Barber sitting just in front of me.

---

6. The Curtis Institute opened on October 1, 1924. Apparently Max Aronoff, the violinist who later played in the Curtis Quartet with Cole, was the first student to enroll and Barber was the second. Heyman, *Samuel Barber: The Composer and His Music*, 33.

7. Barber studied voice at Curtis with Emilio de Gogorza from 1926 to 1930.

8. Boyle taught Barber piano in his first year; Heyman, *Samuel Barber: The Composer and His Music*, 31n. But his West Chester piano teacher, William Hatton Green, was more influential; see chapter 1.

9. Jozef Hofmann (1876–1957), Polish American pianist with a phenomenal ear and memory. He was head of piano at Curtis in 1924 and director of the school from 1927 to 1938. He was responsible for various inventions including shock absorbers, from which he apparently made a fortune.

PD Do you think Scalero provided an Italian influence in the period before Barber met Menotti?

OC I can't say it was Italian. It was just a very thorough scholarly approach to composition. Not just "write as you feel—be original!" [*laughs*]

PD Scalero's music is quite forgotten. Did you every hear anything?

OC I think I must have heard something; it was very conventional. Good, you know [*laughs*], but not very interesting.

PD Do you remember Gian Carlo Menotti arriving in 1928?

OC Oh, yes. Very well. I knew him before he knew English. Before he wrote any operas he wrote short stories; he was always writing and creating. [*laughs*]

PD He must have been unusual at Curtis if he didn't speak any English?

OC There were a lot of kids who didn't speak English. There still are. He was fun; he had a good sense of humor and was always lively, a little bit shy.

PD Were Barber and Menotti obviously soulmates at that stage, two composers with much in common?

OC Well, yes. Sam spoke French with Gian Carlo, and I remember they used to spend weekends out at his house with his family.

PD When Barber went to Italy he met the large Menotti family and also the Scaleros?

OC That was some summers later.

PD So Barber studied with his teacher in Italy too?

OC Oh, sure. That was common with my cello teacher, who used to go up to Maine for the summer and take some pupils there. Mrs. Bok provided housing. It was unique, before Tanglewood and Aspen and the other great summer sessions.

PD Do you remember the impact of Barber's uncle, Sidney Homer?

OC According to all those letters quoted in the Heyman book, he must have had a great influence on him. We played a string quartet by Homer at one time. I don't think it was ever published, but Sam very much wanted to have us play it for him. It was a nice sort of conventional piece, attractive.[10]

---

10. Sidney Homer, *My Wife and I* (New York: Macmillian, 1939). 267.

PD   Homer's songs did get published.

OC   He was quite well-known as a song composer.

PD   It's an extraordinary partnership between Barber and Homer. Were you aware of it at the time?

OC   No.

PD   Because Sidney Homer believed absolutely in Barber as a great composer.

OC   A lot of people did. He was very successful winning prizes and so on as a young person. He wrote a violin sonata that he destroyed—the first violinist of my quartet played it. I don't remember what its weakness might have been, but Sam wasn't very pleased with it. I never saw a copy of it.[11]

PD   The String Quartet was written for your quartet. How did it start?

OC   He was writing in Europe on the Prix de Rome and sent me a letter saying, "I've just finished the slow movement and it's a knockout!" And he underlined "knockout!"[12] [*laughs*] The quartet originally had another last movement. We used to play it here and in Europe, and Barber even liked it. But people began to say, "After that slow movement there ought to be something else." And so he discarded the original movement and just recalled some of the first movement. I think that single movement he originally wrote ought to be played in addition to the published form of the String Quartet.[13]

PD   Like the *Grosse Fuge* of Beethoven?

OC   Yes, it's a kind of scherzo movement. Curtis has the music, but Menotti has said that if Barber discarded it then it shouldn't be played. But after he goes, maybe somebody should perform it.

---

11. Barbara Heyman reports: "The third movement of Barber's Sonata in F minor for Violin and Piano was rediscovered in 2006, masquerading under the title page Sonata for Violoncello and Piano. The music turned up in the estate of the Pennsylvania artist Tom Bostell, who had been a boarder in the Barbers' West Chester home. When asked to view the seventeen pages of manuscript, I recognized the first three pages as those that were missing from the autograph of the Cello Sonata at the Library of Congress. The next pages presented clues that led to a eureka moment. The inscription III, Allegro agitato; the date at the end, November 8, 1928, in Barber's hand; the key of F minor and a sudden awareness that the solo instrument could only be a violin affirmed, much to my delight, that the third movement of the 'lost' violin sonata had been found!" E-mail to the author, July 13, 2009.

12. Compare Heyman, *Samuel Barber: The Composer and His Music*, 153.

13. See ibid., 150–59.

PD   Did you have any inkling that the *Adagio* was going to be an incredibly famous piece?

OC   We didn't know that a slow movement of a string quartet would have that stature! [*laughs*]

PD   Can you suggest why it's become so popular, with eighty-five different versions in the record catalog?[14]

OC   Unbelievable. I know they sing it, they play it for winds and brass—everybody plays it. It's a wonderfully moving and beautifully constructed piece. What sent it off was that Toscanini performed it with full strings. I guess all they did was have Sam add some bass parts to it.

PD   They do make a difference.

OC   Sure, when you have that much volume of strings. I still like it just for string quartet. It's like having fifty people recite a Hamlet soliloquy—it doesn't make it better! [*laughs*]

PD   Did you feel that the orchestral version had taken it away from you?

OC   No. People were always interested in hearing it. We played it in Europe when we traveled with a program that included Sam's quartet. That was before it was famous, but critics picked up on it and usually mentioned it.[15]

PD   What happened about the Violin Concerto?

OC   This young violinist, Iso Briselli, was brought to this country by Carl Flesch when he was twelve in the first year of Curtis—a remarkable violinist who'd given a recital in Berlin that was a great success.[16] Flesch said Iso could be the greatest violinist in the world! He played the whole repertoire. Flesch left after four years, and Iso then studied with Zimbalist and Leopold Auer, and somehow he just didn't progress.[17] The concerts got less and less frequent, and Mr. Fels[18] asked the violist of my quartet, Max Aronoff, what he could do to stimulate Iso's career. Max said he should have a young composer write a concerto; there would be interest

---

14. In 2005.

15. See chapter 2 for critical responses in England.

16. Carl Flesch (1873–1944). Hungarian virtuoso violinist and teacher who studied in Vienna, Paris, and Berlin and taught at Curtis in the years 1924–28.

17. Efrem Zimbalist (1890–1985). Internationally prominent violinist and teacher born in Russia who started teaching at the Curtis Institute in 1928 and was director from 1941 to 1968. He married Mary Louise Curtis Bok in 1943. Leopold Auer (1845–1930), Hungarian violinist who taught in St. Petersburg and moved to New York in 1918. He was a major influence through his pupils such as Zimbalist, Mischa Elman, Jascha Heifetz, and Nathan Milstein.

in hearing it, and he could have the rights and so on. Max suggested Sam Barber, and they engaged him. The story is well-known.[19] Barber finished the first two movements, but Iso thought there wasn't enough virtuosity for a concerto. When he saw the last movement he said it was impossible to play. Then they got a couple of Curtis kids; they played it.[20] I guess they went so far as to have a court session because Sam wanted to collect the commission. He didn't want to lose that after he'd put so much work into it.

PD   You didn't hear any of the readings through?

OC   No.

PD   He used to call it his *concerto di sapone* because it was commissioned by a soap manufacturer!

OC   Fels Naptha soap was world-famous. [*laughs*]

PD   Did you keep in touch with Barber over the years?

OC   Yes, but my quartet traveled a lot in those days and he was living in New York, but for a time he came to Curtis and taught.[21] Then I saw him and had a couple of pupils play the Cello Concerto for him.

TW[22] Did he ever consult with you about writing for the cello?

OC   When he wrote the Cello Sonata he would write three or four pages, and then we'd try it. I was in on that as it was composed, and I gave the first performance of it in New York with Barber playing the piano. He was an excellent pianist. We played it many times for anybody who was interested in hearing it—at Curtis, at the Art Alliance here in Philadelphia.[23]

TW   Do you remember anything specifically? Anything technical?

18. Samuel Simeon Fels (1860–1950), president of Fels and Co.—the manufacturer of Fels Naptha soap—and a philanthropist who supported music. Iso Briselli (1912–2005) was his adopted son who went on to a successful professional career.

19. See Heyman, *Samuel Barber: The Composer and His Music*, 191 et seq.

20. Herbert Baumel played it at two hours' notice and was accompanied by Ralph Berkowitz. See ibid., 193.

21. From 1939 to 1941 Barber commuted from New York to conduct the Madrigal Chorus, and in 1941–42 he taught orchestration.

22. Thomas Winters, assistant professor of music history, West Chester University College of Visual and Performing Arts, West Chester, who recorded this interview.

23. The official premiere was on March 5, 1933, at a League of Composers' concert in New York.

OC   He wanted to have the scherzo that interrupts the slow movement in 12/4 time. As it's very hard to read and know where the beat is in twelve equal quarter notes in the bar, it's much easier if you do it in eighth notes. He changed it to four groups of three notes. That's a minor thing—it didn't change the music at all. There weren't any technical problems. He never wrote anything that wasn't playable or didn't sound good. I think he had had some cello lessons when he was very young.

PD   Did he consult you about the Cello Concerto?

OC   No, that was written for Raya Garbousova and commissioned by John Nicholas Brown in Providence.[24] She was in on the composition of that: it was rather unfortunate that he committed some very difficult things.

PD   I was going to ask you about those double thirds in the first movement.

OC   And there are a couple of very fast light arpeggios in the last movement that are very hard. I remember asking Piatigorsky, "Do you ever think of playing the Barber?" He responded, "Oh those turds, those turds!"[25] [*laughs*]

PD   I can remember that Charles Turner told me they were planning to go to a performance of the Cello Concerto in Detroit. Barber was going to suggest some alterations, but there was a snowstorm and they never got there, so he never made the alterations at that time.

OC   I had a couple of students play it for him; they did quite well and he was pleased. He said: "Why don't cellists play my concerto? It's one of my favorite pieces." I said, "Well, those thirds are so hard." So he took my piano part and wrote "trumpets," then "cello," then "trumpets."[26] It could be reorchestrated to be helpful. But nowadays young people play it. The standard of cello playing has gone up so much.

PD   So it doesn't affect the issue now?

24. Raya Garbousova (1905–97). Russian cellist whose teachers included Felix Salmond and Pablo Casals. She moved to the United States in 1927 and gave the premiere of Barber's Cello Concerto, op. 22, with the Boston Symphony/Koussevitsky on April 5, 1946.

25. Gregor Piatigorsky (1903–76). Influential American cellist, born in Ukraine, for whom composers including Prokofiev, Hindemith, and Walton wrote concertos. He moved to the United States in 1940 and was head of cello at Curtis from 1941 to 1949.

26. See Tim Janof, "Conversation with Orlando Cole," ICS Exclusive Interview, June 14, 2002, including music examples, at http://www.cello.org/Newsletter/Articles/cole/cole/cole.htm.

OC No. Lynn Harrell is performing it, and he's just crazy about it.[27] He thinks the slow movement is one of the greatest things ever written for the cello. Zara Nelsova recorded it in London with Barber conducting—that's a fine job.[28]

PD He was very pleased with that.

OC Oh, sure. And he took some conducting lessons ahead of time. [*laughs*]

PD What should happen for the centenary in 2010? There have been festivals of the complete works of composers such as Stravinsky and Schoenberg.

OC If there's time to play everything, you could do it. Barber would be more palatable than either Schoenberg or Stravinsky! [*laughs*] I grew up in the period when Schoenberg was unheard, really—his quartets and the trio. People said, "Oh, wait another twenty-five years. Everybody will listen and get used to this music." But we haven't. Schoenberg is not on the concert programs with any frequency.

PD Did you play any Schoenberg?

OC Just the student quartet, which sounded like Dvořák and was written before number one—very well constructed, but it didn't sound like Schoenberg! [*laughs*][29]

PD That's the tradition Barber inherited; Schoenberg moved on.

OC They followed different paths.

PD But he wasn't unaware of Stravinsky—look at the *Capricorn Concerto*.

OC He was well aware of what was going on. I remember playing Barber's String Quartet on a program of American composers in New England at Bowdoin College, Maine. Copland, Quincy Porter, and others were there and they said, "Why do you play Barber; it's such old-fashioned stuff?" But this is what's lasted.

PD Did he have a sense of humor?

---

27. Lynn Harrell (1944–), American cellist who studied with Cole and Leonard Rose.

28. Zara Nelsova (1918–2002), Canadian cellist who moved to England, then taught at the Juilliard School from 1962 until her death. Her recording of the Cello Concerto with Barber conducting was made in London in 1950 and issued on Decca DL-10132 (1966), with various reissues. See Heyman, *Samuel Barber: The Composer and His Music*, 315–17.

29. Arnold Schoenberg (1874–1951), major Austrian composer and theorist who moved to the United States in 1931. Early String Quartet in D (1897).

OC   Yes, but underneath it all he was very serious and maybe suffered, even as a young man, from depression. We didn't think much about it in those days. He was a broad person, not shallow in any way. He had a sharp wit, and I guess people might have thought he was little snooty, looking down on others, but I never felt that way.

UK[30]   He was so glad to escape West Chester, which was very much Quaker, so he needed to get away. His trips to Philadelphia were necessary for him to keep his sanity. People in West Chester whom we've interviewed in the past said he was a bit standoffish. They never forgave him for escaping from West Chester, and people there have a long memory![31]

OC   I think they appreciate him now. They didn't then when they wouldn't have known what a composer was.

TW   Do you remember him talking about that at all?

OC   No, not really. I think I met his sister once there.

TW   I suppose we should ask you if you remember him being at all hampered by his homosexuality.

OC   I never remember him being worried about it, but we suspected it when he and Gian Carlo became such a close couple. In those days we didn't know much about it. It wasn't commonly talked about.

TW   It didn't hamper his relationship with Curtis?

OC   Oh, no. He and Mrs. Zimbalist [Mary Louise Curtis Bok] were very close, and she helped him financially in many ways. She did practically anything he asked for and sponsored Gian Carlo's operas. That relationship was very helpful and very necessary.

PD   Do you think being gay affects Barber's music in any way?

OC   I don't think so. They are very productive people and very valued. I'm the older generation, but I never heard any criticism of him that was colored that way.

PD   What about Barber's attitude to religion?

OC   I don't remember that he spoke about it at all.

PD   But he played the organ in church.

OC   I know he had some organ lessons at Curtis.

---

30. Ulrich Klabunde, who kindly arranged this interview.
31. See chapter 1.

UK He was a church organist before he went to Curtis—and got into trouble with the authorities.[32]

PD So did Bach, who was also regarded as old-fashioned.

OC I remember how handsome he was! Goodness!

---

32. According to Nathan Broder, Barber was fired because he "refused to play fermatas when none were indicated in the hymns and responses." *Samuel Barber* (New York: G. Schirmer, 1954), 12.

Selected Bibliography

This is not a complete bibliography. Theses are not included, and there are useful lists in *Samuel Barber: A Bio-Bibliography* by Don A. Hennesee; *Samuel Barber: The Composer and His Music* by Barbara Heyman (1992); and *Samuel Barber: A Guide to Research (Composer Resource Manuals)* by Wayne C. Wenzel. References to *The Times* (London), of which there are many in chapter 2, can be accessed at *The Times* Digital Archive 1785–1985 (archive.timesonline.co.uk/tol/archive); they are not given separately here. However, other relevant British sources are noted since they would otherwise be impossible to trace. Reviews in *Gramophone* can be accessed at www.gramophone.net. In 2009 Pierre Brévignon started Capricorn: l'association des amis de Samuel Barber in France; its Web site is www.samuelbarber.fr.

Alberge, Dalya. "Samuel Barber in Search of Identity." *Performance* 3 (Summer 1981): 16–18.

Anonymous. "London Music." *Musical Times* (December 1950): 482.

———. "New Music." *Musical Times* (December 1941): 430.

———. "Obituary: Hans W. Heinsheimer Dies at 93: Top Publisher of Classical Music." *The New York Times*, October 14, 1993.

———. "Obituary: John Browning." *The Times* (London), March 7, 2003.

———. "Obituary: Gian Carlo Menotti." *Daily Telegraph* (London), February 3, 2007.

———. "Obituary: Gian Carlo Menotti." *The Times* (London), February 3, 2007.

———. "Obituary: Mr. Samuel Barber." *The Times* (London), January 26, 1981.

Ardoin, John. "Samuel Barber at Capricorn." *Musical America* (March 1960): 4, 5, 46.

———. *The Stages of Menotti*. Garden City, NY: Doubleday, 1985.

Ashley, Tim. "A Grand Performance: Samuel Barber's First Opera." *Guardian* (London), November 14, 2003.

Barber, Samuel. "Birth Pangs of a First Opera." *The New York Times*, January 12, 1958.

———. "On Waiting for a Libretto." *Opera News* 22 (January 27, 1958): 4–6. Also in *Contemporary Composers on Contemporary Music*, ed. Elliott Schwartz and Barney Childs. New York: Holt, Rinehart, and Winston, 1967, 165–69.

See also Barber interviews with Emily Coleman, Allan Kozinn, and Philip Ramey in this bibliography.

Bernstein, Adam. "Obituary: Opera's Gian Carlo Menotti; Popular Composer of *Amahl*." *The Washington Post*, February 2, 2007.

Blixen-Finecke, Baroness Karen von [Isak Dinesen]. *Seven Gothic Tales*. London: Putnam, 1934.

Blyth, Alan. "Samuel Barber, Peter Dickinson." *Daily Telegraph* (London), January 25, 1982.

Brévignon, Pierre. *Samuel Barber ou le malentendu*. Paris: Bleu nuit editeur, forthcoming.

Broder, Nathan. "Current Chronicle." *Musical Quarterly* 36 (April 1950): 276–79.

———. "Current Chronicle." *Musical Quarterly* 44 (April 1958): 235–37.

———. "Current Chronicle." *Musical Quarterly* 49 (January 1963): 94–97.

———. "The Music of Samuel Barber." *Musical Quarterly* 32 (July 1948): 325–35.

———. *Samuel Barber*. New York: G. Schirmer, 1954.

Cobbe, Hugh, ed. *Letters of Ralph Vaughan Williams 1895–1958*. Oxford: Oxford University Press, 2008.

Coleman, Emily. "The Composer Talks with Emily Coleman . . . Samuel Barber and *Vanessa*." *Theatre Arts* (January 1958): 68, 69, 86–88.

Copland, Aaron. *Copland on Music*. New York: Doubleday, 1960.

———. *Music and Imagination*. Cambridge: Harvard University Press, 1952.

Copland, Aaron, and Vivian Perlis. *Copland: 1900 through 1942*. New York: St. Martin's, 1984.

———. *Copland since 1943*. New York: St. Martin's, 1989.

Crichton, Ronald. "London Music." *Musical Times* (March 1963): 192.

Daniel, Oliver. *William Schuman*. BMI catalog, 1973.

Demuth, Norman. *Musical Trends in the Twentieth Century*. London: Rockcliff, 1952.

Dexter, Harold. "Samuel Barber and His Music." *Musical Opinion* 858 (March 1949): 285–86, 859 (April 1949): 343–44.

Dickinson, Peter. "American Beauty: Samuel Barber's Concertos for Violin, Cello and Piano." *Gramophone* (April 2001): 31–33.

———. "The American Concerto." In *A Companion to the Concerto,* ed. Robert Layton. London: Helm, 1988, 305–25.

———. "Obituary: Samuel Barber." *Musical Times* (March 1981): 193.

———. "Obituary: Virgil Thomson." *Independent* (London), February 3, 2007.

———. "Obituary: William Schuman." *Independent* (London), February 24, 1992.

———. "On the Trail of Samuel Barber." *Schirmer Repertoire* 8 (May 1982): 6–7.

———. "Record Reviews" (*Vanessa*, RCA Red Seal RL 02094–2). *Musical Times* (October 1978): 864.

———. "Samuel Barber." In *New Makers of Modern Culture*, ed. Justin Wintle. London: Routledge, 2007, 93–94.

———. "Stein Satie Cummings Thomson Berners Cage: Toward a Context for the Music of Virgil Thomson." *Musical Quarterly* 72, 3 (1986): 394–409.

Dickinson, Peter, ed. *Copland Connotations: Studies and Interviews*. Woodbridge, Suffolk: Boydell, 2002.

Dyer, Richard. "Antony and Cleopatra." *New World Records* 80322–2 (1984).

Edwards, Sidney. "Paste amid the Diamonds: Sydney Edwards at the Opening of the New Met." *Music and Musicians* (November 1966): 20–21.

Ericson, Raymond. "*Vanessa*—the New Samuel Barber Opera." *Opera Annual* 5 (1958): 116, 125–27.

Ewen, David. "Modern American Composers." *Musical Times* (June 1939): 413–16.

Eyer, Ronald. "Premiere of Barber's *Vanessa*." *Musical America* (February 1958): 5, 126.

Friedberg, Ruth. *American Art Song and American Poetry. Vol. III: The Century Advances*. Metuchen, NJ: Scarecrow, 1987.

Gelatt, Roland. "Opening Night at the New Met." *High Fidelity/Musical America* (November 1966): MA-8–MA-10.

Goodwin, Noel. "Samuel Barber: Spitalfields." *The Times* (London), July 7, 1980.

Grange, Henri-Louis de la. "D'Amérique, un compositeur Américain independent." *Contrepoints* 4 (May-June 1946): 65–66.

Greenfield, Edward. "Lyrical Notes: Edward Greenfield Pays Tribute to the American Composer Who Has Died at the Age of 70." *Guardian* (London), January 26, 1982.

Griffiths, Paul. "Record Reviews" (Violin Concerto). *Musical Times* (October 1978): 864.

Gruen, John. *Menotti: A Biography.* New York: Macmillan, 1978.

Harewood, Lord. "The New Met." *Opera* (November 1966): 843–44.

Harrison, Max. "Music in London." *Musical Times* (November 1972): 1099.

Heinsheimer, Hans W. "Adagio for Sam." *Opera News* (March 14, 1981): 30–32.

———. *Best Regards to Aida.* New York: A. A. Knopf, 1968.

———. "Birth of an Opera." *Saturday Review,* September 17, 1966, 49–50, 56–58.

———. *Fanfare for Two Pigeons.* New York: Doubleday, 1952.

———. *Menagerie in F Sharp.* Garden City, NY: Doubleday, 1947.

———. "*Vanessa* Revisited." *Opera News* (May 1978): 23–25.

Heyman, Barbara B. Samuel Barber: A Documentary Study of His Works. PhD diss., City University of New York, 1989.

———. *Samuel Barber: The Composer and His Music.* New York: Oxford University Press, 1992.

———. "The Second Time Around: Barber's *Antony and Cleopatra* at the Lyric Opera of Chicago." *Opera News* (December 7, 1991): 56–57.

———. "*A Comprensive Catalog of the Complete Works of Samuel Barber,* forthcoming.

Hennesee, Don A. *Samuel Barber: A Bio-Bibliography.* Westport, CT: Greenwood, 1985.

Hitchcock, H. Wiley, with Kyle Gann. *Music in the United States: A Historical Introduction.* Upper Saddle River, NJ: Prentice-Hall, 1969, 1974, 1988, 2000.

Hixon, Donald L. *Gian Carlo Menotti: A Bio-Bibliography.* Santa Barbara: Greenwood, 2000.

Holland, Bernard. "Gian Carlo Menotti, Prolific Composer of *Amahl* and Other Operas, Dies at 95." *The New York Times,* February 2, 2007.

Homer, Sidney. *My Wife and I.* New York: Macmillan, 1939.

———. *Seventeen Songs.* Compiled by Samuel Barber, with a preface. New York: G. Schirmer, 1943.

Horan, Robert. "American Composers, XIX: Samuel Barber." *Modern Music* 20 (March-April 1943): 161–69.

Hull, Robin. "Broadcast Music." *Musical Times* (October 1958): 546.

Jackson, Richard. "Samuel Barber." In *The New Grove Dictionary of American Music,* ed. H. Wiley Hitchcock and Stanley Sadie. London: Macmillan, 1986, 142–47.

James, Henry. *Roderick Hudson.* London: Penguin, 1969 [1874].

———. *Washington Square.* New York: Harper and Brothers, 1880.

Kaufman, Louis, and Annette Kaufman. *A Fiddler's Tale—How Hollywood and Vivaldi Discovered Me.* Madison: University of Wisconsin Press, 2003.

Kozinn, Allan. "Musicians of the Year: Samuel Barber." *International Music Guide* (1981): 10–14.

———. "Samuel Barber: The Last Interview and the Legacy." *High Fidelity* (June 1981): 43–46, 65–68; (July 1981): 45–47, 80–90.

Lane, John Francis. "Obituary: Gian Carlo Menotti." *Guardian* (London), February 3, 2007.

Leichtentritt, Hugo. *Serge Koussevitzky: The Boston Symphony Orchestra and the New American Music.* Cambridge: Harvard University Press, 1947.

Marcus, Michael. "Successes and Failures at Salzburg." *Music and Musicians* (October 1958): 11–13.

Maw, Nicholas. "Choral." *Musical Times* (August 1961): 508.

McNaught, William. "Gramophone Notes." *Musical Times* (May 1945): 149.

———. "Gramophone Notes." *Musical Times* (October 1948): 304.

Mellers, Wilfrid. *Between Old Worlds and New.* London: Cygnus Arts, 1997.

———. *Caliban Reborn: Renewal in Twentieth-Century Music.* London: Gollancz, 1968.

———. "Gramophone Records." *Musical Times* (November 1965): 867.

———. "Language and Function in American Music." *Scrutiny* (April 1942): 346–57.

———. *Music and Society.* London: Dennis Dobson, 1946.

———. *Music in a New Found Land.* London: Barrie and Rockcliff, 1964.

———."Music in the Melting Pot: Charles Ives and the Music of the Americas." *Scrutiny* (March 1939): 390–403.

———. "New English and American Music." *Scrutiny* (Spring 1943): 168–79.

———. "Samuel Barber at Seventy." *Records and Recording* (July 1980): 31–32.

———. "Searchlight on Tin-Pan Alley." *Scrutiny* (March 1940): 390–405.

Mitchell, Donald. "London Music." *Musical Times* (August 1955): 433.

Mitchell, Donald, and Hans Keller, eds. *Benjamin Britten: A Commentary on His Works from a Group of Specialists.* London: Rockcliff, 1952.

Norris, Geoffrey. "The World's Favourite Opera Composer: Gian Carlo Menotti." *Daily Telegraph* (London), March 7, 2002.

Oja, Carol J. *Making Music Modern.* New York: Oxford University Press, 2000.

Pears, Peter. *Travel Diaries 1936–1978,* ed. Philip Reed. Woodbridge, Suffolk: Boydell, 1995.

Polisi, Joseph W. *American Muse: The Life and Times of William Schuman.* London: Amadeus, 2009.

Porter, Andrew. "Antony's Second Chance." In *Music of Three Seasons: 1974–1977.* New York: Farrar, Straus and Giroux, 1978, 97–102.

———. *Musical Events: A Chronicle 1980–1983.* New York: Simon and Schuster, 1987.

Ramey, Philip. "A Talk with Samuel Barber." *Songs of Samuel Barber and Ned Rorem.* New World Records NW 229 (1978).

———. "A Talk with Samuel Barber." *Third Essay for Orchestra.* New World Records NW 80309-2 (1981).

Rockwell, John. "A Conversation with Virgil Thomson." *Poetry in Review* (Spring-Summer 1977): 417–35.

Rorem, Ned. "Samuel Barber." In *A Ned Rorem Reader.* New Haven: Yale University Press, 2001, 238–45.

Rouse, Christopher. *William Schuman: A Documentary.* New York: Theodore Presser and G. Schirmer, 1980.

Rutland, Harold. "Thomas Schippers." *Musical Times* (March 1957): 157.

Sackville-West, Edward. "A Quarterly Retrospect: April-June 1951." *Gramophone* (August 1951): 9.

Sadie, Stanley, ed. *The New Grove Dictionary of Music and Musicians.* London: Macmillan, 1980.

Salter, Lionel. "Review: Decca X305." *Gramophone* (June 1950): 14.

Schonberg, Harold C. "Vladimir Horowitz." In *The New Grove Dictionary of Music and Musicians,* 2nd ed., ed. Stanley Sadie. London: Macmillan, 2001, 222.

Simmons, Walter. *Voices in the Wilderness.* Metuchen, NJ: Scarecrow, 2004.

Tawa, Nicholas. *American Composers and Their Public: A Critical Look.* Metuchen, NJ: Scarecrow, 1995.

Teachout, Terry. "He Brought Opera to Broadway: Gian Carlo Menotti, R.I.P." *The Wall Street Journal,* February 3, 2007.

Thomson, Virgil. *American Music since 1910.* New York: Holt, Rinehart, and Winston, 1971.

———. *The State of Music.* New York: Vintage Books, 1962.

———. *Virgil Thomson.* New York: A. A. Knopf, 1966.

Tischler, Hans. "Barber's Piano Sonata, Op. 26." *Music and Letters* (October 1952): 352–54.

Tommasini, Anthony. *Virgil Thomson: Composer on the* Aisle. New York: Norton, 1997.

Wenzel, Wayne C. *Samuel Barber: A Guide to Research (Composer Resource Manuals).* New York: Routledge, 2001.

Williams, Ralph Vaughan. *National Music.* Oxford: Oxford University Press, 1934.

Wittke, Paul. "Samuel Barber: An Improvisatory Portrait," 1994. www.schirmer.com.

Zeffirelli, Franco. *Zeffirelli: An Autobiography.* London: Weidenfeld and Nicolson, 1986.

General Index

Index of Works by Samuel Barber

Samuel Barber is one of America's most popular classical composers. His works—including "Adagio for Strings" and *Knoxville: Summer of 1915*—have been regularly performed and recorded all over the world. The centenary of his birth, in 2010, is a landmark that will confirm his position as one of the great creative spirits of the twentieth century.

The main source for *Samuel Barber Remembered: A Centenary Tribute* is a panoply of vivid and eminently readable interviews by Peter Dickinson for a BBC Radio 3 documentary in 1981. The original BBC program lasted an hour, but the full discussions with many of the main figures connected with Barber have remained unpublished until now. These include Barber's friends Gian Carlo Menotti and Charles Turner; his fellow composers Aaron Copland, William Schuman, and Virgil Thomson; performers with whom he worked closely such as Leontyne Price (soprano), John Browning (piano), and Robert White (tenor); the historian H. Wiley Hitchcock; and publishers Hans W. Heinsheimer and Edward P. Murphy.

The book also offers three of the very few interviews extant with Barber himself, as well as a discussion with cellist Orlando Cole, one of the first students to enter the Curtis Institute with Barber in 1924. Most of the interviews were given to Peter Dickinson but others involve James Fassett, Robert Scherman, Allan Kozinn and Arthur Johnson.

Dickinson contributes two substantial chapters: one on Barber's early life (drawing upon historic interviews recorded by Brent D. Fegley and others) and another on Barber's reception in England. The book has a foreword by the distinguished composer and admirer of Barber, John Corigliano.

Peter Dickinson, British composer and pianist, is emeritus professor, University of Keele and University of London, and has written or edited numerous books about twentieth-century music. *CageTalk: Dialogues with and about John Cage* (University of Rochester Press) was hailed by the *Times Literary Supplement* as "the ideal introduction to John Cage." Dickinson's other books include three published by Boydell Press: *The Music of Lennox Berkeley*; *Copland Connotations*; and *Lord Berners: Composer, Writer, Painter*.

"As a biographer, I find Peter Dickinson's beautifully annotated book of interviews an indispensable resource. Dickinson, a composer himself, brings a unique perspective to the interviews: his penetrating questions yield a vivid and sympathetic portrait of Samuel Barber through the eyes of those who knew him best—friends, performers, lovers, his publisher, and colleagues."

—Barbara Heyman, author of
Samuel Barber: The Composer and His Music

"A unique and valuable addition to the existing literature on a remarkably gifted musician. British musicologist Peter Dickinson applies his considerable talents to create a scholarly and absorbing portrait of Barber, as he has done previously with Copland and Cage. *Samuel Barber Remembered* brings together the memoirs of many who knew and worked with Barber, among them Leontyne Price, William Schuman, and Gian Carlo Menotti. The result is an absorbing and intimate portrait of one of the finest creative musical figures of our time."

—Vivian Perlis, biographer of Aaron Copland;
founding director of the Oral History,
American Music archive at Yale School of Music